More Praise for Raul Hernandez Ochoa and *Productive Profits*

"Raul has the rare combination of having both depth and breadth of skills, combined with the patience and passion to help others. He's particularly good at helping people streamline and codify their internal business processes in order to scale."
— Victoria Griggs, CEO of Straight Line Marketing

"Compassion | Creativity | Confidence... those are the three words I'd use to describe Raul. Raul keeps the main thing, the main thing. He's invested in people, and knows that when you take care of people, the results, the money, the success all follow. No use having all the skillsets in the world if that same someone can't implement, take proactive action, make judgment calls and do the heavy lifting if need be. Raul will do what is necessary, and there's nothing I am drawn to more than confidence. Raul is someone you want to work with if you want results and an experience."
— Dr. Galen Detrik, CEO & Co-founder of The THRIVE Dentists

"Raul is an amazingly supportive teacher and coach. He encouraged me, welcomed my questions, listened to my frustrations, helped me learn from my mistakes, helped me define my strengths, and gave me advice that I literally still have taped on my laptop. He is definitely using his superpower to help others find theirs"
— Tracy Rye, Instructor at AdSkills.com

"I love the way Raul's mind works. He has the unique ability to make order and systems in places I see complete chaos."
— Mike Zimov, Founder of Clickstorm LLC

"Raul has a charismatic and systematic way of explaining situations that would otherwise seem complex and unfathomable. He has a unique process driven yet philosophical approach to business and enterprise. A rare combination in a world of the cookie cutting coach. Having seen Raul speak on stage and have the privilege to speak with him in person as a friend. It is no surprise to me that Raul would write such an incredibly well presented and pragmatic book on business FOR business owners."
— Lee Brooker, Digital Marketing Consultant & Strategist

"Systems….systems…systems. Raul hates this word but he's a genius at systems that help you scale income while reducing stress and workload. It's so clear to me what I need to automate, outsource, and do myself. He's helped remove me from MOST of the tasks in my business, automate with people/tools, and grow a TRUE lifestyle business."
— Sean Kemp, Creator of Doctor Framed

"I love the way it reads conversationally and still gets valuable points across. It's like speaking to a consultant in person and not reading a book."
— Mark P. Jacob, Director of Operations at CFO Hub

"Raul is a great business coach. He helped me become clear on what value I bring to my target market, where to reach them, and what message I should deliver. He helped me create a step by step plan on how to market to my clients and how to measure how well things are going."
— Jason Carter, PhD, Machine Learning Software Engineer

"Raul brings the human element and says, okay 'let's talk about you, your goals, your business, your ideas, your customers, your mindset '- all these

different elements. That's where the secret sauce is, being able to bridge the gap between the data of the numbers, the raw intel that you need to run an effective business and have great systems AND also the emotion, the human components. Raul really does a phenomenal job with that, his results speak for themselves."
— John Nemo, CEO of Nemo Media Group

"Raul's method is a must for business owners, especially ones that lean toward a more creative mindset instead of an analytical one. This book helps businesses build a solid foundation by following an incredible amount of actionable insights. The book could be mistaken for a business plan and is a blueprint to proven, consistent success. Use the book as a tool to scale your new business the right way, all the way to the success you have envisioned. Here is your road map."
— Justin Darby, Owner at Justin Darby - State Farm Agent

"If I could recommend only one book on growing a business, this is certainly a book that I would recommend. I'll be adding it to my resource list as a book recommendation to coaching/mentoring clients, fellow entrepreneurs and anyone who wants to save themselves time while growing a business."
— Eustan Matthews, Business Strategist & Coach

"Productive Profits simplicity cuts to the heart of what you need to do to really scale your business. This book has given me clarity and helped me identify the bottlenecks in my business (usually me). I am now creating evergreen workflows and delegating more tasks than ever!"
— Charles Alexander, Business Owner

"Come ready to work with Productive Profits! Raul leads you on your own empowerment journey through a profound series of questions and Action Maps, chapter by chapter building on your own personal insights. The more you give of yourself in the early self-discovery insights, the more you will get out of the later scalable processes. Raul simplifies the complex hidden business traps through his authentic, transparent, and qualified experience. Productive Profits does more than impact your business. It will impact you towards success in every facet of life you are Called-To."
— Jody Matheson, Creative Strategist

"Whether you run a large company or you are a solopreneur, this book will give you insights on how to maximize your company's impact and how to streamline all processes. This is one of the best books that I have read on this topic. Raul writes in a very clear, concise way and invites us to ask very empowering questions. One of the things that I loved most about this book was the way he moulded the action map at the end of each chapter. A must read for all those who are serious about growing their business and their impact in the world."
— Barbara Vercruysse, Entrepreneur & Corporate Leader Coach

"Productive Profits is a must-read for any business owner. Not only does Raul personally give you the roadmap you need to succeed as a CEO, but he also does it in a way that takes your business on the journey it needs for maximum impact."
— Brandon Clark, Partner at Bristers Online Stores

About The Author

Raul Hernandez Ochoa is a business strategist, coach, and consultant. He has trained hundreds of entrepreneurs through live seminars, online programs, and private masterminds. He's played a key part in helping scale businesses and has overseen hundreds of online advertising campaigns. His work has helped positively impact the lives of his clients and the teams he's helped flourish.

He lives in San Diego and is loving life with his family. When he's not working and drinking a homemade cold brew coffee, he's either serving his community and Church, training for a crazy obstacle course race, or simply surfing.

Get Your Free Bonuses at:
dogoodwork.io/book-bonuses

PRODUCTIVE PROFITS

The Founder's Guide To Scaling Your Impact

RAUL HERNANDEZ OCHOA

Copyright © 2020 by Raul Hernandez Ochoa
All Rights Reserved.

ISBN: 9798622669934

Gabriela & Johnny, thank you for your constant encouragement and the sacrifices you've made for us to have a solid opportunity to follow our dreams: "Echale ganas, Rulo".

Don Raul, thank you for everything you have done for us.

Diego, you help me be a better brother. I love you.

Tracey, you're my amazing support.

AMDG

ACKNOWLEDGEMENTS

There is no such thing as a self-made person. I wouldn't be here without the Grace of God in the gift of my life. I aim to live fully and give fully of my gift while I still have breath in me.

I'd like to acknowledge the men and women who have directly and indirectly impacted and helped me shape the development of this book.

The first goes out to my mentor and most importantly good friend John Morgan who saw something in my work and encouraged me to fulfill my potential to serve more entrepreneurs. I am extremely grateful for you planting the seed and continual support and encouragement.

John Daniel Martinez, man, thank you for helping me push my physical and mental limits with all of our crazy endurance training and events. Your discipline and mental strength is something I look up to and has served both me in my work and my clients.

Ricardo Ceceña, thank you for your admirable support in putting in extra time to help me learn English when I first arrived in the United States and walked into your second grade classroom. I'll never forget the impact you made for me and my family.

Dr. Carmen Carrasquillo Jay, thank you for seeing something in my writing style in your college class and "nudged" me to go the extra mile to be part of the honors curriculum. You showed me that with a little extra effort one can stand out and perform at a different level with driven individuals.

Jenny Amaraneni, thank you for being an inspiration in helping me see that one person can make such a global impact through business. Your story opened my horizons to pursue entrepreneurship as a path in life.

Leonard Lavin and family, I thank you for your extreme generosity and gift to San Diego State University in developing a world class entrepreneurship program. This program literally changed my life. Alex DeNoble and Bern Schroeder, thank you for not only the instruction you gave all of us but also the exposure, opportunity, and immersion in entrepreneurship in the community. This program was the ultimate college experience.

Kanstantsin Sandovich, thank you for introducing a scholarship program to the foundation and helping me get involved with my first experience in global entrepreneurship. I'll never forget our early startup days.

Rory Stern, thank you for investing in my growth.

Heather and Jason Hornung, thank you for fostering my growth and exposing me to coaching, training and supporting entrepreneurs worldwide.

Sean Kemp, thank you for your support and for showing me how to communicate my protocol in an easy and digestible way.

Aaron Parkinson, thank you for the trust and responsibility you gave me to help you grow a world class team and brand.

CONTENTS

ACKNOWLEDGEMENTS	vii
A NOTE FROM THE AUTHOR	x
FOREWORD	xi
INTRODUCTION	1
WHY I WROTE THIS BOOK	2
WHAT IS PRODUCTIVE PROFITS	4
CHAPTER 1 THE SUBTLE QUESTION THAT WILL EMPOWER ALL YOUR ACTIONS	6
CHAPTER 2 EASILY KNOW YOUR COMPANY'S PULSE AT ALL TIMES	12
CHAPTER 3 REACHING YOUR HORIZONS	30
CHAPTER 4 HARMONIZING YOUR MISSION, VISION, AND VALUES	41
CHAPTER 5 OPTIMIZING YOUR TEAM FOR GROWTH	47
CHAPTER 6 BALANCING YOUR CEO 80/20	62
CHAPTER 7 REDUCING WASTE AND MAXIMIZING YOUR COMPANY'S ACTIONS	71
CHAPTER 8 DESIGNING YOUR EVERGREEN FLOWS	78
CHAPTER 9 SCALING YOUR IMPACT THROUGH HEROIC LEADERSHIP	94
CHAPTER 10 ORCHESTRATING YOUR GROWTH	106

A NOTE FROM THE AUTHOR

Your ability to grow & scale is in direct proportion to how well you run your company.

After training and consulting hundreds of entrepreneurs in growing their businesses and playing a key role in helping multi-million dollar companies scale, I've packaged everything that has gotten me results into the simple protocol that I now use to help my clients reach new levels of success, clarity, and impact. This book is that protocol and I hold nothing back.

I can't wait to hear how it's helped you on your journey.

Do Good Work,

FOREWORD

How can someone be both creative and analytical? This was the question running through my mind when I first met Raul. Most entrepreneurs seem to lean one way or the other. Raul can excel at both. From the moment we met, I've been impressed with his knowledge and inspired by his deep passion for helping people.

Having built a company that ran without me thanks to strong workflows, I thought I knew systems and processes. When I started working with Raul, I realized there was a lot I didn't know. It became clear his method of creating evergreen workflows would allow businesses to scale quickly and safely. Simply put, he can see what others cannot.

It's more important than ever that a business becomes able to grow with proper workflows. Customers get better, more predictable service . They receive better results. Employees are able to do better work and enjoy their job. And you, the business owner, can achieve your goals without sacrificing your family, vacations, and hobbies.

Isn't that why you started a business to begin with? You want to serve others and build a great life for your family. Too often, this becomes an either-or scenario rather than a both scenario. To build a great business, you must be able to use your unique skillset, gifts, and talents. But you have to be able to scale those things.

For over a decade, I've had the pleasure of working with entrepreneurs. These entrepreneurs have been women and men. Small business and some large brands. Some have been young and some have been older. Regardless of their background, industry, or where in the world they live, they all have one thing in common: they want to impact the world.

So how do you impact people and do it at a high level? How can you build something that allows you to do what you do best while equipping others to play a role in your vision?

You're about to find out.

What Raul has developed is a method and framework that stands on a foundation of strong principles and solid strategy. Don't just read this book. Study it. Put in place what you learn. Your business will transform and you will be able to focus on impacting others and fulfill your calling.

    — John Morgan,
        author of bestseller *Brand Against The Machine*

INTRODUCTION

We tend to think that our business is unique and different from the herd. It's not our business that is truly unique but our impact.

Impact begins with you, the founder: your fire, ideas, tenacity to go to market and solve a problem in a unique way, breeding life into a company. Your impact does not end with you. It extends to those closest around you and finds its way to your team, shareholders, vendors, and relationships.

It's found in the way you do business, the way you treat others, and the feeling you create in your customers, namely your brand, and your team (your culture). To quote St. Teresa of Calcutta (Mother Teresa), "love begins at home." Your impact begins with you. As your impact spreads into the community you begin to increase your reputation, thus increasing your reach. To the point where you are now making your mark on the world to the extent that you desire. Isn't this why we started in the first place?

As business owners, we must watch our impact as we watch our bottom line since they go hand in hand. Value, profits, and opportunity compound as we increase our impact. But we must do this in an intelligent way. A balanced way where we can truly scale our impact without compromise.

This is my goal for you.

WHY I WROTE THIS BOOK

In my experience working with entrepreneurs, coaching leaders, helping teams grow and flourish, I observed a *key inflection point* that occurs when businesses have a certain level of momentum and reach a certain level of success.

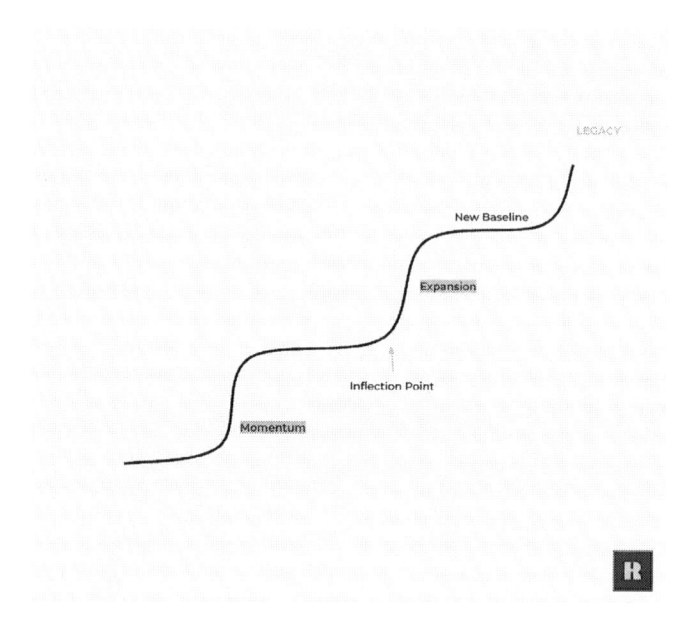

Legacy

New Baseline

Expansion

Inflection Point

Momentum

The point of inflection occurs when a business goes through what I call a "stress test." As the business works to grow past this point, hidden weaknesses of the business begin to surface and the strength of the company's infrastructure determines if this next level of growth will be a slow one, a negative one, or a smooth ride.

The purpose of this book is to empower business owners like you to successfully maintain success past these points in growth and build an even more solid foundation (the new baseline) so you can continue to expand your impact and leave a legacy that can live on.

Productive Profits™ is the accumulation of real world experience and results. This book is written how business *should be*: **simple**.

Each chapter will cover a specific principle within the Productive Profits protocol, detailing why the principle is important and then give you an action map that will help you easily implement what you learned immediately after finishing each chapter. You'll notice each page has a sidebar section for you to write down your own notes and action items.

As you implement what you learn in this book, my hope is that one day you'll be able to say "*I have Productive Profits in my business.*"

WHAT IS PRODUCTIVE PROFITS

Productive Profits™ is the protocol I created and used to help business owners reach new levels of success, clarity, and impact.

Productive Profits does not *only* mean profit for your bottom line but profit that changes lives. As a business owner, it will profit your mindset by relieving the stressors and frustrations of feeling "trapped" in your business. It will also profit your team as they have a clearer and more enjoyable path of working towards success. Your family and friends will also profit since you won't be married solely to your business and will have the leverage to allocate your time as desired. Most importantly, your *impact* will profit as you will be able to **expand** what you're able to do in your business as well as outside your business... so you can leave the legacy you were created for.

Typically when you think of a "formula," "method," or "protocol," you may imagine it be a series of stages that progress top-down, in a linear fashion, with a beginning and an end. I would like you to change that way of thinking...

Productive Profits is a *cycle*.

There is only a beginning but there is no finite end. How is that? Ask yourself, *"Is there any point where you achieve perfect excellence?"*

We are in a constant process of refinement, always becoming better, continuing down the path of excellence. Productive Profits helps you and your team travel that path.

The work we do with Productive Profits is ever evolving, moving one step closer to *better* and adapting to the current state of the team, the business itself and the business environment as a whole, at the present time.

As Daft Punk says in "Harder, Better, Faster, Stronger": *our work is never over.*[1]

Productive Profits has three distinct stages. These stages are holistic and work in tandem creating a harmony that is adaptable to businesses and teams of various sizes since it is founded on principles.

The three phases are:
1. Clarity
2. Evergreen Flows
3. Sync

What we will do for the remainder of the book is dive into each phase and give you a clear action map so you can apply these principles immediately.

---

[1] Daft Punk. (2001). *Discovery*. Virgin Records (Recorded 1998-2000).

CHAPTER 1
THE SUBTLE QUESTION THAT WILL EMPOWER ALL YOUR ACTIONS

As we focus on building a solid foundation for your business to reach new levels of success, we need to set parameters in order to maintain our focus and efforts. As visionaries and creatives, when we focus on solving a problem, all options and solutions can be, quite literally, endless. Having too many options can cause overwhelm and lead to no solution being implemented. This is why it is important to define parameters first so we can align our thinking and energy.

The first parameter we will set is to review what type of business track you're on. Everything that you will build moving forward will fit within this parameter.

Let me explain:

Let's say you are building a lifestyle business where your business allows you to live a certain way. For example, the business can allow you to travel, explore new places or help you live a lifestyle where you can be around your family and witness your children's first words.

Or perhaps your business track is focused on high growth/maximum payout, looking to sell and exit the business in the next X amount of years. Typically this track is demanding on the business owner and team, can lead to longer hours invested at work, and takes place in a fast paced work environment.

These are just some examples of the types of tracks you can be on, but it's important to be self aware of what track you are on because the foundation you build will be to support this track.

So let me ask you: what track are you on?

As you identify the track and set this first parameter, let's next focus on the types of actions you're taking currently in your business…

Our actions are influenced by our priorities and our priorities are set by our values. If we have a clear set of values, we have our priorities set and our aligned actions that follow. But our priorities may not always be as clear as we'd like them to, especially when facing multiple demands within our business. This is where the **questions** we ask ourselves come into play. Our priorities can become clear when we ask the right types of questions.

Most entrepreneurs when planning the next quarter, year, or stage in their business tend to ask a very basic question:

"What do I want?"

This question is almost always tied to a revenue goal or a numerical growth number (i.e. X amount of new users by Y date).

Now, this is not a bad thing to do. We've all been there. However, this is a very basic question that has some drawbacks.

For example, what if *what* you want changes? Is it a seasonal want? Will it change when your attention focuses on something new?…

You also have to ask several follow up questions to "what do I want". The famous follow up question tends to be: *"WHY* do I want that?". Now you have to try to connect what you want to a priority you have in your life and business. Sometimes that can be clear, sometimes you have to make up some weird logic like a high schooler making up fake math to solve a calculus question they were not ready for...

If that wasn't enough, there is typically another follow up question... one that has you second guessing yourself when you pose a response to "what do I want":

"Do I *really* want that?"

Let's recap this logic string:

"What do I want?" leads to "WHY do I want that" which concludes with self-doubt: "do I really want that?"

Asking "what do I want?" can have entrepreneurs going in circles questioning themselves with a plethora of follow up questions. To add even more complexity to the situation, try imagining how this debate can drag on within large leadership teams in a company.

Nevertheless, the question "what do I want?" or "what do we want?" is not a bad starting place. Most companies can and do reach success through such questions.

However, I encourage you to **ask better questions** that are in line with your values and go straight to the heart of your priorities in less time and with more clarity. One such question is:

"What am I Called-To?"

Notice this subtle shift in perspective. At first glance, it doesn't seem much different... but this question has helped teams and leaders lay the groundwork of a much more solid foundation in their life AND business to truly reach their goals. And that's exactly what I want you to do.

Now, in full transparency, there are no perfect questions, however, asking "what am I Called-To" or "what are we Called-To" does have its advantages.

In order to answer the question, you and your team need to have a certain level of self awareness of 1) your current reality and 2) the current state of the business.

This is important to note because it doesn't allow you to shy away from the current responsibilities you and the business are facing - even though there may be stressors and headaches to deal with.

Asking "what am I Called-To" also forces you to step outside of yourself, your comfort, and focus on impact. When you are thinking in line with your responsibilities, priorities and values, your attention is driven to ultimately focus on the impact of the work you are doing. And if you are focusing on impact, you are focusing on value. And the more value you deliver to your current customers or to potential customers, the more revenue your business will generate.

When you focus on impact, you will not only reach revenue or growth numbers faster but you will do it in a much more empowering way, especially **when** the going gets rough. Not if. When.

How?

A clear defined set of values and priorities that is shared with your team helps develop a vision. This vision of the company is driven by your mission for impact. Reinforcing your vision and mission creates your company culture. Showing your team that they play a vital role in the overall vision and helping them develop in their roles to support the mission builds a dynamic atmosphere where your team will fight alongside you and not just work for you. (We will dive deeper into your mission, vision, and values in Chapter 4.)

All of this is driven by and stems from what you are Called-To.

I was visiting my buddy's office in Old Town on a late and warm San Diego afternoon. We had just gotten back from eating a late lunch and were talking shop. Our talk led to some of the goals we were tracking to hit in our businesses. We noted some of the differences we had in our business goals and lifestyle. The conversation sparked a story my friend knew of two well known marketing entrepreneurs in San Diego who started similar companies but who went down very different journeys. One grew his company that allowed him to maintain the lifestyle he wanted. He was content with the growth and size of his company which brought him to roughly 20 employees. The other expanded his company to other cities and grew to the point of getting acquired by a global company that has allowed them to expand their team to over 20 countries. I will never forget how my buddy ended the story "to each, his own".

There is no wrong answer but there is also the possibility of not living your potential. With so many opportunities and choices, we must not take our power to choose for granted. We must get out of our own way and go directly to the core of what we ought to do.

To recap, asking "what am I Called-To?" leads you to focus on your values. These values reveal your priorities and power your company's mission and vision. Reinforcing your mission and vision nurtures your company culture and your key habits that drive the actions you take to reach your goals and create a greater impact.

ACTION MAP

What are you Called-To?

Take some time, ideally 1 hour, on your own to review all areas of your life and the goals you have in each area. Step away from your normal work environment and spend some time alone. A pen and notepad is recommended here.

When focusing on your business, take a good look at where you currently are at and ask yourself: "what am I Called-To?"

If you lead a team with other decision makers in the business, ask them to do the same on their own.

Once everyone has a clear idea of what they are Called-To, create space in your schedule to meet together and have an open and collaborative discussion. This may take place over several sessions, ideally no more than 3 to 5 separate sessions.

*Review one another's answers and see how it resonates with the mission and values of the company. If the answers are aligned with the mission and core values, begin to come up with creative ideas on **how** and **when** these Called-To goals can be applied.*

If they can be applied immediately, take action to do so without delay. If not, keep your initiatives in a backlog and review them in your next team planning session when going over your upcoming month, quarter, or year.

Chapter 2
Easily Know Your Company's Pulse At All Times

When I speak to entrepreneurs and go through the Called-To exercise with them, they are fired up and excited about what the future holds. Then the conversation shifts to "where do I start?!"

It's time to roll up our sleeves. Now that you know which direction you want to go, it's important to assess your company's current State of the Union in detail.

I like to put it like this:

As your eye looks toward the horizon (your goals), your fingers must be on your company's pulse.

So let me ask you:

What's the pulse of your company right now?

If you cannot answer that question within 3 to 5 minutes, we have some work to do.

In this chapter we are going to review the baseline pulse of your company so we can better understand your current situation. This will help us know exactly what actions we need to take in order to reach the goals we are Called-To accomplish.

When I review the baselines of my client's company, I like to look at two key aspects of their business: their **team** and their **numbers**.

Your Team

Let's review your team together.

Team Roles & Responsibilities

When looking at your company's team I want to understand how your team functions, how the team coordinates initiatives, how the team communicates, and how the team takes action. I'm looking for what makes your team great and at the same time, what makes the team not so great.

Diving in a bit further, let's break down each individual role and see how each role plays a part in the overall company strategy and mission.

Next, let's dissect the responsibilities each role carries. Each team member must have specific responsibilities and goals to meet in order to succeed. If you don't have specific goals or milestones, how will you measure success?

Lastly, we need to understand if each person is in the **right** role for their skill sets and personal character traits.

Now, if you are a small team or a team of one, I understand that there's a lot of hats being worn by one or multiple people. So why bother thinking of all these roles and responsibilities now?

As your company scales, so do your roles.

Having predefined roles and responsibilities makes it easier for you to assess, plan, hire and place the right person in the best role in your company's future.

The reason why I ask for such detail is I'd like you to be in a position where you can tell me at any given moment what the next three to five smartest and best decisions are in your company. If you can't answer that right now, ok, we'll work together in the exercises for this chapter's Action Map to get you there. If you can, you're where you need to be.

Remember: *eyes to the horizon, fingers on the pulse.*

Team Performance Reviews

Now, as you review your team, what mechanisms do you have in place to review their performance? How do you measure your team's success?

We will need to know transparent metrics the employee and you can review in order to measure progress or lack thereof.

This is important for two reasons:

First, if there is a lack of results in a team member or department, immediate action needs to be taken in order to address it. As a leader, when you review the cause of the lack of performance, you need to look at yourself. Is the team well equipped with both the resources and training to succeed? Could you have caught the issue sooner with tighter feedback loops?

Second, if a team is performing well or above expectations, how can you reward them? Keep in mind rewards don't always come in monetary form such as salary increases or bonuses. For example, you can have additional access to personal and career growth resources, recognition, or help them create a new roadmap to advance in their position or greater role in the future.

Team Communication

Next we review your team's communication.

Your team's communication will most likely fall into one of these four major communication categories:

- Strategic
- Edifying
- Action oriented
- Fun/team building

Within any of these communications there is transmission of information. It is your responsibility to discern what information must be saved for later use, implemented immediately, or disregarded if it holds no value to your company mission, your team, or your wellbeing.

One of the biggest gaps I work to close in my own teams and clients' teams is **the gap between information and action**. You and I will work on this together as we review how your team communicates with each other, how information is passed along and what mediums your team uses to communicate.

To start, answer the following questions:

Does your team have a centralized port for communication? Where is communication happening?

When there is essential information communicated, where does your team store it and can it be easily accessible when needed?

How do you keep track of your team's key initiatives and actions?

As the leader, you own the entire process of your team's communication and must know what initiatives your team is working on *at any given time.*

Let's say you and I were to hop on a virtual conference call and on that call I asked you: *"What are the top three things your marketing department is doing right now, who is doing them, where are they in the process and when is the estimated time for completion?"* Could you give me an answer within 3 minutes?

The only way you can develop such an oversight is by developing dashboards for key initiatives your company undertakes. Creating such dashboards will allow you to keep your finger on your company's pulse *automatically*. Better yet, as you develop these dashboards, you can train your team to sustain them so you get a State of the Union for every key aspect of your company within minutes.

Some key dashboards you must have in place are: financial dashboards, team roster dashboards, marketing and sales dashboards, project dashboards, and client fulfillment dashboards.

The tools in which you create these dashboards are irrelevant. It is not the tools that you use that matters, but how you use them. However, I do get the question a lot of which tools to use. My answer depends on the type of company you run, the number of team members you manage, your industry, goals, and business track that you're on.

But here are simple parameters I use when deciding on what tool to use for myself and my clients:

- Does this tool fit my budget?
- Does this tool fit my current needs?

- Does this tool scale as my company grows?
- Do I like using this tool?
- Can my team easily learn how to use this tool?
- Can I see my team use this tool 5 years from now?
- Can I train my team in using this tool?

As you develop dashboards for every key initiative in your company, always keep in mind that the dashboard must be fluid, adaptable, and easily accessible to the people on your team who need it. Don't create dashboards that widen the gap between information and action through clutter, confusion, or lack of use.

Team Culture

The last key area I take a look at when we analyze your team is your culture. How do team members treat one another? How are they communicating? What do they think of the company as a whole and, most importantly, what do they think about their role in the company? What habits do you have in place to support the vision and values of the company?

As the leader, it's your responsibility to tend to your team. Not only must you work to achieve your company's mission and goals, but you also must do so in a manner that the team is driven to support the mission and goals of the company and work alongside you (not just for you). Their experience matters. Keep in mind that alone you will not be able to accomplish everything with the same efficiency as with your team.

The vision of a Productive Profits™ team is one that works holistically and in line with the overarching goals of your company. People are happy to go to work, have positive interactions with their peers, and work on challenging yet rewarding tasks together. They are also willing to go to battle with you and for you, standing by your side as you lead the company to growth and expand the company's impact.

There is a difference between having a team who's just working *for you* versus a team working *with you*. The difference is incredible and having a positive team culture makes any difficult mountain to climb much easier to summit.

I remember when I introduced a company training agreement with a fast growing team I ran. The company invested in some of the top training programs in the industry and our goal was to have select team members sign an agreement to commit to stay at least 6 months with the company if they were to have access to the training. At the same time, we were building a growth oriented and supportive team culture unlike what was common in the industry. To my surprise, the team culture we were breeding was more powerful than I thought. Since this was a new agreement, I reached out to each member individually to introduce it. One of our team members responded in a way I was not expecting... "you're asking for 6 months? I'll give you 6 years!" As time went on, her actions reflected her words and her commitment only grew stronger.

Your Numbers

Now that we have reviewed what I call the soft side of your company, utilizing soft yet essential skills, let's step into parts of your company that only tell the cold truth: your metrics.

Every company that I have worked with has their own specific key performance indicators for success metrics. Your metrics are different than mine. However, we do share commonalities. What we will be dissecting in this section are the overarching numbers that you care about when reviewing your company's overall health and performance. These are the exact same metrics I review when taking a first look at my client's internal operations.

First, let's review your profit and loss reports over the last 6 months. Ideally, we will review your P&L broken down by customer or services rendered. Most top accounting tools allow you to do this, if not, please request this report from your accountant.

From a bird's eye view, your P&L shows us what your biggest revenue drivers are, where your largest expenses are coming from, what trends are happening month to month, and if you are on track to reach your next milestone goal. You'll be able to identify the growth speed of your company and also identify immediate waste in expenses. Sometimes it's better to cut the waste first in order to move and grow at a faster pace.

With a closer look, what we want to dive deeper on is who our highest value customers are and what services are we offering them. We do this for two reasons:

1. We want to identify if our highest value customers and highest value services align with where we invest our resources, team, and time.
2. We want to be able to formulate new ideas for services offering to either better cater to our highest value customers or create more high value customers.

Next, let's review your sales and marketing pulse:

How long does it take for prospective customers to go through their journey of getting to know who you are and making a buying decision?

How long is your sales cycle?

How can you shorten your sales cycle?

How can you provide more value to prospects in the sales cycle?

How can you iterate the sales cycle to be more cost-effective?

What does your sales forecast look like?

Do you have a proper pipeline and deal flow that you can measure and predict how many customers will inflow by the end of this month and the upcoming month?

Diving deeper we want to look at your profitability metrics. These are three key metrics I look for:

1. Your cost to acquire a new customer
2. Average value of a customer at their first point-of-purchase
3. The lifetime value of your customer

These numbers will help us understand the true value of your customers, the highest value customer segments in your business, and your customer's journey.

Let's have a closer look at the key metrics listed above and ask questions that can allow us to increase the value of our current customers and strategically lower our costs to serve MORE customers.

Your Customer Acquisition Costs

Are you currently spending money to acquire customers? This can be done through many paid channels to acquire customers such as media, advertising, promotions, events, and so on. If not, perhaps you are spending your time and effort through networking, relationship building, content creation and the like. Regardless of what route you have taken, we need to assess a true cost (in time or money) of acquiring a new customer in your business.

But knowing the cost is not enough. We must understand your threshold costs to make economical sense. For example, let's say you are selling a $500 service and currently it's costing you $750 to get one customer. Can this business maintain itself? At first glance, no it cannot, if the business is overspending to make a sale and is not breaking even.

So in your business, what is the cost you need to be below to acquire a new customer?

A simple way of looking at it is:

Price
- Cost to Deliver Services
- Desired Profit Margin
= Ideal Cost to Acquire a New Customer <u>for that specific service</u>.

Let's say the $500 service you are selling costs you $200 to deliver and you want to keep 30% profit margin ($150). Your ideal cost per acquisition for that specific service is $150. That means you can spend up to $150 to get one customer to buy that service.

Looking at the same example, there are instances where paying $750 for a customer to purchase a $500 service makes economic sense. To do that we must look at our average order value and customer lifetime value.

Average Order Value Per Customer

If your business is only marketing to sell one product and only get one sale from each buyer interaction, you are leaving opportunity on the table. If, however, when you engage with buyers, you present your buyers with more value and opportunity to buy from you, you have a higher chance of increasing your average order value and profit. Your customers win because you offered to increase the value they receive from you. You win because you were able to increase profits from that single interaction.

So when your customers engage with you as a buyer, you want to look at your customer journey and identify where you can add offers to increase the value you deliver to your customers. Doing so not only increases your bottom line but it also allows you to have more leverage in the marketplace and stay competitive.

Increasing your average order value allows you to increase your acceptable cost for acquiring a new customer.

For example, if you place an offer after customers purchase your $500 service for a related service or product, a bundle or a downsell, you will be able to increase the average amount your customers spend thus increasing your average order value. Let's say your average order value is $800, the cost to deliver your core service is $200, the cost to deliver a related service is $100, and you want to keep a 30% profit margin from the average order value; the formula then becomes:

Average Order Value ($800)
- Cost to Deliver Services ($200 + $100)
- Desired Profit Margin ($240)
= Ideal Cost to Acquire a New Customer for that transaction is $260

In the previous example, we could only spend $150 to sell our $500 service. Now, we can spend upwards of $260 to sell the exact same service with an additional offer during the buying experience that got us a higher average order value. Not only did we increase profits from adding an additional offer but we also added more value to your customers. Not to mention, we now have an $110 dollar difference that you can leverage.

With those additional dollars you have several options. Here are the main two:
1. Keep the additional profits
2. Invest the additional profits to acquire more customers. (This route will also allow you to invest in other marketing and sales channels that you may have not been able to afford in the past.)

In your business right now, what opportunities are you missing out on to drive more profits and add more value to your customers?

Lifetime Value of Your Customer

If the average order value looks at the initial transaction in your customer's journey, then lifetime value looks at your customer's second, third... fifth... twenty first transaction!

In other terms, you've already asked them on the first date and it went well. How are you strengthening that relationship as time goes on?

Do you know your customer lifetime value?

If not, start now. Looking at your revenue metrics, P&L and customer relationship manager, establish a rough value for your CLTV (customer lifetime value). Go as far back as you can, but six or even three months is a good time frame to measure.

Just how knowing and increasing your average order value gives you leverage, knowing and working with your CLTV gives you a long term strategy. This is how spending $750 to make a $500 sale makes economic sense.

Following the same example, if you know that your customers spend upwards of $3,000 with you during the first three months of your relationship, spending $750 to get them in the door as a customer may make sense depending on the business model.

As we take this back to your business, we want to be looking at your customer journey and identify where we can add more opportunities for your customers to get more value and buy from you during the lifetime of your relationship.

Highest Leverage Marketing Channels

As a capstone, we want to now view your marketing efforts and see which initiative is driving in the most customers and the highest quality customers to your business. We already know which metrics we look for to determine our highest value customers, now we need to identify what actions your company is taking to increase the volume of customers as well as which actions bring in the highest value customers.

We do this by reviewing your marketing channels. Which channels are you currently using to reach your customers? Circle the ones that apply and write down any not listed here.

- Paid Advertising
- Social
- Direct
- 1-on-1
- Referrals
- Email

These channels allow the customers to get to know you, establish a relationship with you, and eventually purchase from you. Which of these channels are bringing in the bulk of new customers? Which channels are bringing in your highest value customers?

Now, as you identify your highest leverage channels, take a good look at where you currently invest your time and effort with your marketing. Is your company's actions aligned with the highest value channels? If not, now you know what needs to change.

Facilitate Scale

As you assess your company's State of the Union and review the two key aspects of your business (your team and numbers), you will have a more accurate pulse of your business.

But it doesn't end there.

With your eyes to the horizon and your finger on the pulse you can clearly see what you need to do in order to have the right resources, people, and teams in place to reach your Called-To goals.

Doing so will allow you to facilitate your company's growth. There is no better place to be in your company than facilitating and orchestrating growth. If you are stuck in the day-to-day operations of your company, read on. These upcoming chapters will show you how to focus your time and energy on the highest leverage activities for your company and mission that will help you become a facilitator of growth.

ACTION MAP

Area of Focus: Your Team's Roles & Responsibilities
List out every person on your team and:
1. *Assign a clear role title*
2. *Write out your vision of an ideal team member's behavior in this role*
3. *Describe how this role plays a vital part in the overarching company mission (you want to continually reinforce this with each team member because one way of keeping talented individuals on your team for the long term is allowing them to see themselves in the company's future)*

4. Detail what metrics/milestones you will keep track of to measure success in this role
5. List out the key responsibilities that this role entails
6. List out what resources, access, and credentials this role needs to succeed
7. List out the important meetings this person needs to be a part of

NOTE: The exercise above works great and will give you more clarity when you are creating new positions in the company and are looking to hire new team members.

Area of Focus: Your Team's Performance
Ensure you have a habit of reviewing your team's performance on a frequency that suits your company (monthly, quarterly, or semi-annually). There should be an electronic record of the answers given during a performance review as well as a 1 on 1 meeting with the team member and their supervisor to discuss their performance.

Here are my general guidelines for what you want to measure prior to the performance review meeting:
- Team member's experience with the company
- Team member's confidence in the company and the team
- Team member's perception of the mission, vision and values
- Ensure team member's role is clear to them
- Ensure team member is clear with team communications
- Ensure team member has a sense of fulfillment at work, see that their work makes an impact, and has a healthy work/life balance.
- Include accomplishments team member is proud of
- Include areas team member can improve
- Include the team member's suggestions for the company: what to do more of, less of, and stop doing.
- Ask the team member what they want more from the company

- *Have the team member rate themselves on a performance rating scale in the following areas:*
    - *Company Values*
    - *Work Approach*
    - *Teamwork*
    - *(Add any area you see fit)*

To measure, I suggest using the 5 level performance rating scale:
1. *Exceeds Expectations*
2. *High Meets Expectations*
3. *Meets Expectations*
4. *Low Meets Expectations*
5. *Needs Improvement*

As you review your team member's responses, set time to meet with them 1-on-1 for 20 to 30 minutes to discuss and give them your analysis of their work performance. This meeting should conclude with action items on both sides, yours and theirs, in order to improve the overall company environment.

Area of Focus: Your Team's Communication
Create the following:
1. *A centralized location where all team communication can happen between team members and the entire company*
2. *A centralized location where important files and documents are kept for your team's reference*
3. *A dashboard where you can see your team's key initiatives, progress, and open action items so you can determine the State of the Union within minutes of any given project happening within your company*

Area of Focus: Your Team's Culture
- *List out your company's values*
- *With each value, list out or create habits that support each value you stand for and reinforce the value within your team*

Area of Focus: Your Company's Numbers

Review your company's profit and loss statements for the last 6 months and identify:
- What expenses you can cut
- What services are generating your highest value customers
- Can you create/add new services to increase value for your highest value customer?
- Can you create/add new services to increase the number of customers you serve?

Area of Focus: Your Company's Sales and Marketing Pulse

Customer Acquisition Costs
- How can you lower your customer acquisition costs?
- What are some ways that you can get leads at breakeven costs so that new customers come at a profit?
- How can you outspend your competitors in strategic ways to acquire customers in ways they cannot while still maintaining your ideal customer acquisition cost?

Average Order Value Per Customer
- How can you increase your customer's average order value?
- Can you add similar products or create new offers for your customers at checkout or post purchase?
- Can you bundle products or services to increase your overall average order value at point of sale?

Customer Lifetime Value (CLTV)
- How long is your customer lifecycle?
- What is your CLTV?
- What products/services can you create or package to lengthen your customer's journey and increase CLTV?
- How can you integrate monthly and annual recurring revenue models with current customers?

Highest Leverage Marketing Channels
- *Which marketing channels bring you the bulk of your customers?*
- *Which marketing channels bring you high value customers?*

Chapter 3
Reaching Your Horizons

Now that we have a good pulse on your company we need to act.

Motion.
Action.
Progress.

With the baselines we covered, we have a solid understanding of what needs to change, what needs to be improved, and what we need to put into place in order to reach our Called-To goals. In this chapter, we are going to put everything together and create a plan that will help you truly achieve the goals you set out to reach.

WARNING: This isn't some goal setting workshop.

We're going to dive deep into your Called-To goals and create an actual strategy that will have you approach your goals in a new light that will have you and your team focused on only executing the highest leverage actions in your company. My goal is to help you make success inevitable.

To do this, I'm going to create a challenge for you.

What I have gone and done is put together a simple goal challenge that will incorporate your Called-To goals and convert them into a challenge. I've also sprinkled a bit of brain science, habits, and careful planning into the mix.

What we're going to do for the rest of this chapter is walk step by step through each point of the challenge outline so by the end of this chapter you'll be able to write out your goal challenge and get to work.

Why a challenge?

For me personally, any time that I focus on a goal but don't have a very specific time frame or clear plan set to achieve it, the goal seems to just sit there on the shelf while time goes by...I won't let that happen to you. On my health journey, I've experienced that if I do a weight training program, I can stick to it for years with solid, yet slow, progressive growth. However, the most rapid progress I've made was when I started challenging my mind and body through endurance training and obstacle course races. The subtle shift that occurs when I have a challenge in front of me with an approaching deadline, has me approach my training and discipline differently.

From what I have experienced, when we are faced with a challenge, we can either rise to the occasion, break any barrier separating us from our outcome, or shy away. It is how we respond to challenges that matter. We either rise up or shy away. The beauty of our goal challenge is this is something we have full control over. We can set it on our own terms and set ourselves up to win from the start.

SECTION I
What are you Called-To?

*"I am Called-To {{verb}} **OUTCOME** by **DATE**"*

*Set a goal that stretches you but that you also **believe** you will achieve.*

You'll notice that in the first part of the goal challenge we focus strictly on what you're Called-To do and add a deadline. Not only is it important to set specific timelines in order to reach a goal, it's also extremely important that you **believe** that you can achieve this goal within that timeline. I cannot overemphasize this point.

You need to be honest and review with yourself: "Do I truly believe I will accomplish this goal?", "Is this timeline too generous," "Is this timeline too short," and "Is this a healthy timeline where I can truly see myself reaching my desired outcome?" If you are reviewing your Called-To goals with your team, discuss these questions as a group to assess a realistic yet challenging deadline.

When you are writing out this section of the challenge in the Action Map below, do not go any further from this point until you have firmly set a specific outcome with a specific date and that you firmly believe that the goal can be accomplished. If you do not believe that this goal can be accomplished, you will simply not accomplish it.

SECTION II
Why This Needs To Happen

Next on our challenge, we will work with the motivators and key psychological factors that will anchor you to *why* you need to achieve this goal. Your Called-To goals naturally have emotion attached to it; we are just going to dive deeper. We are going to leverage your emotional attachment to your *reasons why* in order to help you get through any difficult dips that you will ultimately face on our journey to reach your goals. It's not a matter of *if* you will face dips or difficulty but a matter of *when*.

Going back to my endurance training, I know that there is a moment where I will hit a physical or mental wall and will have to strategically work my way through it in order to finish. Now, you may not do endurance training but when you're giving your full effort, especially with goals that you are **Called-To** accomplish, it is going to require you to be the version of yourself that accomplishes the type of feats you set out to do. And you may not fully be that version of yourself yet. This path you're on is going to require change.

Diligence. Effort. Growth.

So before we head over to the next section, I want you to focus and write out three to five different reasons why you need to accomplish your Called-To goals.

Reflect on why you need to accomplish this Called-To goal:

Finish the sentence: "This needs to happen because...   "

SECTION III
Success & Milestone Mapping

This is a fun, simple, and powerful section. First, we are going to visualize what success looks like for you and your team. No, we are not going to "manifest" or "attract" anything here. We are just driving your attention to focus solely on your Called-To goal. That's it.

We do this by uniting your *reason why* emotions to your belief that you can truly accomplish your goal. This will increase your motivation and drive. With this drive and seeing yourself accomplishing your goal you will be able to:

- Plant seeds in your mind to be aware of opportunities in your environment that can help you reach your Called-To goals in ways you haven't planned.
- Motivate those around you, especially your team as you lead them towards success.

But before you can actually visualize success, we need to understand and take note of how you are going to measure success and progress.

The best way to measure success is to map your milestones. In other words, what does the road to success look like? By knowing what milestones you need to reach you can identify progress and celebrate these wins with your team (a reward for taking the right actions) and, most importantly, you can strategically plan the road ahead as you embark on your Called-To mission.

Next, you need to measure progress. As discussed in Chapter 2, you need to have dashboards in place that will allow you to check the pulse of your key company's metrics. Measuring your progress frequently will allow you to know your company's cadence and if you need to improve performance in order to hit your milestones more efficiently (by optimizing your time or resources).

Complete Section III by filling out the exercise below to visualize success and measure your progress:

Success
What does success look like when completing this challenge?

Success looks like:

Milestone Mapping
Milestones I Need To Hit To Complete Challenge
1. *x*
2. *x*
3. *x*

I will measure progress by:

I will measure progress every:

SECTION IV
Your Corner of the Ring & Your Risk Reduction Plan

Next we move to see who is on your corner of the ring.

Any time you go out to do something impactful in your life, something challenging, working towards accomplishing a mission, focusing on something new, helping more people, serving more, increasing your impact... you will ultimately face hurdles that you need to go through or obstacles that you did not foresee. Due to our human condition, complexity of the world we live in, and the reality that the unexpected can happen, we have to plan proactively how we will react if these things happen.

The first step in planning is to take inventory of the people who are fighting alongside you. Those that will help you achieve the goals that you need to achieve. If you currently don't have a person at your side, you will need to take into account who you need to recruit to help you along the way.

No one is self made.

If you need inspiration and ideas of whom you may want to recruit, here are a few considerations:

- Who do you need to hire to help you reach your Called-To goals?
- Who will you need to consult with?
- Who will be on your corner to support you emotionally?
- Who will help you with the mental game?
- Who can introduce you to an opportunity that can support the mission?

These can be people whom you already know or people you will have to find by asking your network.

The second step in planning is to be self aware. We want to have a humble approach and understand our own deficiencies, as well as the business's deficiencies. **This does not mean we accept them as final**. We can and will correct them. We just want to assess, based on our current circumstances, what could go wrong and identify what the triggers or cues look like when something goes wrong.

As you identify these triggers/cues, you will write out an exact action that you will perform in order to react positively to these cues. This is your risk reduction plan that will allow you to mitigate risk, bounce back from negative scenarios faster, and allow you to potentially avoid issues altogether. This self awareness will allow you to catch issues long before they become a problem.

So take the time to prepare your corner of the ring and map out your risk reduction action plan below:

Your Corner of the Ring
List out who will support you, who you need to recruit for support and why they need to be involved:

Risk Reduction Plan
*Plan what things **could go wrong** (cue) and **what you will do to positively counter these things if they happen***

Cue: X
My positive response: Y

SECTION V
Key Habits

So far we know the goals we need to achieve, we've set deadlines that we believe and can see ourselves hitting, we know what success looks like and what we need to measure in order to track success, we understand who we need to have on our side to help us, and we've come up with an action plan for when something goes wrong. Now all that's left is to focus on are the very actions that are required to make achieving our goals inevitable.

Now, I don't want to focus on the minutiae of all the thousand little things you need to do in order to complete your goal. I want you to focus on the essential actions. The actions that will be done consistently over time that will allow you to make miles of progress each and every day.

Consistent actions completed over time are contained in habits. We are going to focus on the key actions you need to take in order for you to develop the key habits to succeed.

These key habits can be done daily, weekly, or monthly. As long as your team focuses its energy and resources towards the *right* actions, the ones that truly drive the company forward, you will achieve your goals.

As you define your key habits, it is essential that you schedule them on your calendar to set aside time to focus on work that falls under each key habit. The work that you do under each key habit is where your current thousand item to-do list exists… But my goal with having you focus on your key habits is to eliminate the clutter of your glorified to-do list.

To show you behind the scenes of my personal and business habits, I have developed a set of eight key habits that allow me to make daily progress in the areas of my life and business that matter most to me.

These key habits also allow me to show up sharp and focused each day in order to drive the mission forward.

My key habits are:

1. Prayer
2. Planning
3. Studying
4. Exercising
5. Coaching and Consulting (delivering my services to the market)
6. Creating (programs, training, videos, podcasts, posts, events, etc.)
7. Connecting (nurturing opportunities, developing strategic partnerships, selling, etc.)
8. Spending time with family & friends

These key habits contain in themselves a wide array yet specific theme of key actions and strategies within them. For example, notice how I have exercise as a key habit rather than a specific workout routine. The routine (or in business: the tactic, strategy, or new flashy thing) lies within the habit. Routines and strategies are interchangeable and can vary by season. These habits, however, rarely waiver. Can they evolve? Yes. But do they change every week? No.

You bet I have time scheduled out for these key habits in my calendar.

Now it's your turn, what are the key habits you, your team, and your company need to harness and hone in on in order to accomplish your Called-To goals?

Step 1: List the Key Habits that are needed to accomplish your goal
1. *Habit*
2. *Habit*
3. *Habit*

Step 2: Schedule your key habits on your calendar to intentionally work on succeeding and reaching your goals

Once you have gone through and created your goal challenge, review it daily. You need to know this by heart so you can focus your attention and actions towards accomplishing what you've set out to do. It will also allow you to refine and make proper adjustments as you move forward.

ACTION MAP

Fill out your complete Goal Challenge and I'll see you in the next chapter.

What are you Called-To?
Set a goal that stretches you but that you also believe you will achieve.

"I am Called-To {{verb}} OUTCOME by DATE"

Why This Needs To Happen
Reflect on why you need to accomplish this challenge?

"This needs to happen because:

Success
What does success look like when completing this challenge?
Success looks like:

Milestone Mapping
Milestones I Need To Hit To Complete Challenge
1. x
2. x
3. x

I will measure progress by:

I will measure progress every:

Your Corner of the Ring
List out who will support you and who you need to recruit for support and why they need to be involved
-
-
-

Risk Reduction Plan
Plan what things could go wrong (cue) and what you will do to positively counter these things if they happen

Cue: x
My Positive Response: x

Key Habits
- Step 1: List the Key Habits that are needed to accomplish your goal
    1.
    2.
    3.

- Step 2: Schedule your key habits on your calendar to intentionally work on succeeding and reaching your goals

Chapter 4
Harmonizing Your Mission, Vision, and Values

Our next step together is to create harmony with your company mission, vision, and values. We have touched on these earlier in the book; however, the reason why we're focusing on this now is because I want you to set your priorities and understand your baselines first. Now we can succinctly solidify your mission, vision, and values and you can clearly see how they harmonize with your Called-To goals and key company habits.

Focusing on your impact, reinforcing your mission, vision, values, and nurturing a strong company culture is all driven by your company's **habits**.

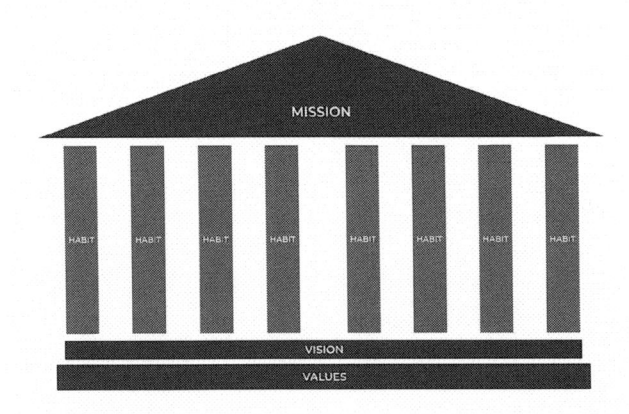

There are many key habits that support each pillar of your company (we will dive deep into them in the following chapters); however, the key habit you can focus on right now is *communication*.

What communication habits do you have in place in your company that reinforce your mission, vision and values to your team, stakeholders, partners, clients, and prospective clients?

These communication habits help your team focus on the right actions that need to take place at the right time so your team can move progressively towards your mission and creating a greater impact in the market and community. Your communication habits also will attract the right type of team members as well as the right type of customers.

Let's dive into a simple exercise to clearly define your mission, vision, and values.

Mission

For your company mission, all you have to do is simply answer the following question: why are you in business?

Answer this with a maximum of two to three sentences. You can move on to the next section only once you've answered this question in three sentences or less.

Vision

We've discussed your vision earlier in your goal challenges, but now I want you to think broader, I want you to think bigger, and holistically...

What is the ultimate impact your company is aiming for?

What does that impact look like next year from now?

How about 3 years from now?...

Now, let me push you a little bit towards the edge: what does your impact look and feel like 8 years from now and 21 years from now?

Don't be afraid to think big and don't worry if you don't have all the answers.

I just want you to write down the adjectives, visuals, feelings and emotions of what the impact you're working to create looks like for the people you serve.

The more detailed you can describe your impact, the better you can communicate it to your team, shareholders, partners, and market. The more clear you can communicate your vision, the more others will understand it and either want to be a part of it or support you on your journey towards it.

Values

Holding firm on your values is attractive. You will attract those who share the same or similar values as you. Doing so will allow you to hire those who are ready to take on your values and attract opportunities that support your values.

What do you stand for?

What will you never tolerate?

It is as important to know what you do not stand for as much as knowing what you do support.

As you detail your company values, you must ensure you currently have key habits in place right now within your company that support your values. If you do not have key habits that support your values, which ones can you develop?

The next step is to articulate clearly your mission, vision, and values to your team. You will do this both verbally and by the actions you take as a leader. All of this creates your company culture and brand.

This foundation branches out to your:

- Language and feel of your marketing
- Client's perception of your company
- Internal team's communications and behavior

...all driven and focused on increasing your impact.

ACTION MAP

Complete the following Mission, Vision and Values exercise:

Mission
Why are you in business? In 2-3 sentences max.

Vision
What does that impact look like? Look at a 1 year, 3 year, 8 year and 21 year perspective to give you inspiration.

Values
What do you stand for?

What will you never tolerate?

What habits support your values?

What communication habits do you have in place that communicate and reinforce your mission, vision and values to your team, stakeholders, partners, clients and prospective clients? Start by bringing this question up at your next leadership team meeting and brainstorm how you can communicate your mission frequently to your team.

Creatively Communicate Your Mission, Vision, and Values

You want your team, partners, shareholders, clients and prospective clients to know and understand what your company mission, vision, and values are. Doing so will reinforce the message, cultivate a better team culture, attract the right team members and clients and bring about new opportunities.

Brainstorm creative ways you can integrate your Mission, Vision, and Values in your company's:

- *Work environment. For example if in a physical office: murals. If in a remote work environment, having your mission, vision and values pinned and visible in centralized team communications.*
- *Brand: collateral, website, emails, and social media*
- *Interactions with your shareholders, prospects, and customers*

Chapter 5
Optimizing Your Team For Growth

More often than not, especially in high growth startups, the founders, CEOs or COOs, (whatever title they choose) wear more than one hat and play multiple roles in their company. Maybe that's you. While this may be good in the short term by keeping you agile, able to pivot quickly and learn fast, as the company grows, as your impact expands, you simply can no longer be the bottleneck of your company's growth and impact.

Bottlenecks are anything that are stunting, hindering, or slowing down your growth and ultimately limiting the impact you create for your team, customers, marketplace, shareholders, community, and family. If you want to reach your Called-To goals this year, next year, 5 years from now and even 20 years from now, bottlenecks must be eliminated.

Are you the biggest bottleneck in your own business?

As we discussed in what I look for when reviewing my clients' teams in Chapter 2, you should now have clearly defined roles and responsibilities for everyone on your team. In this chapter we are going to take things a step further, building off of the foundation you built and streamline your company to eliminate bottlenecks in your team while keeping you agile and able to grow and learn fast.

Do you have the right people in your team?

I've been the founder of small startups, part of the leadership and C-suite in different companies. If there is one thing that is constant in business, it's that you have to work with what you got as you make the transitions and moves to be where you ideally want to be. My philosophy has been to maintain the baselines and keep what's working ON in order to meet short term responsibilities while working towards reaching my horizons.

As I like to put it: you always have to keep the fire of the train engine going while at the same time build the train tracks up ahead to your destination. You might not agree with my management style but the way I see it, the train never stops.

In my experience leading different teams, you get a sense of who is capable of meeting their job responsibilities, who has potential, and who you have to keep a close eye on. I want you to review your team right now as if I were in your office sitting at the table with you; I want you to tell me you have a bulletproof team working with you.

You may have a full team with every job role filled but can you guarantee this is the team that is going to help the company reach the next milestone? Is this the team that actively drives the mission when you're not there? Do you have the right people in the right roles on your team?

How do you find out?

There are several ways, here are a few:

- The quality of the actual work being done. You measure this through success metrics, performance reviews, and active communication with your team members.
- Personality and behavior assessments. For example does your team member's personality or behavior profile match up with the ideal profile for their role? There are many personality and behavioral tests; however, the one I use and recommended for hiring is the DISC assessment because it creates awareness of the behaviors certain team members have and will empower you to plan which behaviors are ideal for specific job roles and foster a positive work environment that meets your team's needs.

- Your team member's attitude towards work and other team members. Remember this: a teammate's positive attitude is not easily replaceable. If you think you can train a negative attitude out of one of your team members, you are in for a long and difficult road. I prefer hiring someone with a positive attitude with medium skill sets but with the potential to grow into their role over someone with a poor attitude yet highly skilled.

As you grow, it is essential that you continue to assess and refine the quality of your team. Not every hire you make will work out. I've made great hiring decisions and helped team members flourish in their role by developing their skill sets. On the flip side, I have made some bad hires and made the mistake of not firing team members who weren't cut out for their role fast enough.

I want you to benefit from the good I have been able to create in the teams I've led and also learn from my errors. One of the most important things I've learned in leadership is that you will make mistakes. The faster you learn to accept that, the faster you can act to course correct. I will show you how to avoid bad hires in your team but that's not enough. You also need to know the signs of when to let a team member go. My hope in describing these telltale signs is to allow you to make a decision faster so you don't waste time like I have.

Before we get into these 4 telltale signs, I'd like to share with you two points that have helped me make executive decisions faster.

Point 1:

A team member is either contributing to or taking away from the company's mission and impact. The whole purpose of the company is to create impact and if your team member is limiting your impact or throttling the overall mission, they should not be there. It is not in the best interest of the mission. Keeping them on the team is tolerating mediocrity. As a leader, you are only as good as what you tolerate.

Point 2:

A mentor shared with me his story of when he took too long to let someone go. When he eventually fired the underperforming team member, they responded "I'm surprised you didn't do it sooner." The moral of the story is if someone is underperforming and not a good fit for the role, they know it. And unfortunately, there are some employees who just wait around until something happens. Going back to point 1: you cannot tolerate mediocrity.

The 4 Telltale Signs

I reflected on the team members I had to let go over the years and analyzed the characteristics and behaviors that led up to them being let go. I've condensed these behaviors into 4 telltale signs that can help you discern if a team member is cut out for their role.

Here are the 4 telltale signs to consider letting go of a team member:

1. They lack communication and delay response time.
2. Creating excuses early on in the relationship as to why they are not getting work done.
3. They lack initiative, lack follow up, and miss deadlines.
4. They persist in making the same mistake repeatedly after several interventions and corrective meetings.

Keep in mind that as I share these pointers and telltale signs, you must have taken action steps to correct issues before they become bigger problems. You must always ask yourself:

- "What have I done to prevent this from happening?"

- "How can I communicate in a more clear way so my team understands and takes the right actions?"
- "What workflow or training can I put in place that will eliminate this issue from happening again?"

Course Correction

As important as it is to have team onboarding processes, it is just as important to have a clearly defined path for leaving the company. The first step towards this clarity is to have a termination policy in place with your company and communicate that policy with the team.

Here's a sample termination policy and the message I use to communicate the policy with the team:

As part of the leadership team, terminating team members is the last thing we want to do (and hope to never have to). However, it is important that we communicate with you what our process is when situations arise where we need corrective action and if that corrective action is not applied by team members.

Yellow Flag: Warning to take corrective action

Red Flag 1: Corrective action was not taken/ team member violated our team policy to a greater degree

Red Flag 2: Final red flag before termination

Red Flag 3: Termination

If you set your company's expectations clearly continually support your company culture and values through your company habits - then someone who continually breaks:

1. Job expectations
2. Core company values

... is essentially *firing themselves*.

If someone violates a highly important company value or policy at will and knows what they are doing, they should be fired immediately. No exceptions.

If you are on the fence of letting a team member go and you can answer "yes" to all of these questions, the issue is not with you but the person performing the work:

- Did I give this person enough support or opportunities to step up in their role?
- Did I clearly communicate their job expectations in ways they understood and confirmed they understood?
- Did I clearly articulate our company values to this individual and did I confirm their firm understanding of them?

Course correcting your team can be hard. To make things a bit easier for you, here is my process for firing a team member:

1. Set a time to meet with the individual
2. Ask them if they know why you are meeting with them
3. Let them know they no longer have a place with the company and why
4. Let them know that their actions dictated your decision
5. Let them know their last day of work and next steps
    - If you discern that their behavior after receiving the news may be disruptive to the entire team, remove all access to company assets and let them go immediately.

After you have let a team member go you must offboard them from your company. Part of your offboarding process must be removing them from payroll, removing their access to key software/tools/logins, and removing them from team meetings and communications.

Your Team Thriving

As a leader of the team, your main focus needs to be on nurturing your team, fueling their growth, and cultivating their happiness (happy individuals are roughly 12% more productive[2]). These following habits are applicable to every team regardless of your brand, culture, and values; they are transcendent.

Good team members want to be nurtured with:

- Challenging yet fulfilling work
- Professional development
- Opportunity for growth in their current role or new roles
- Feeling valued by upper management and by their team
- Support to fulfill their role from the company
- Opportunities for increase in pay

Notice that I put monetary incentive last.

Although money plays a vital role in attracting skilled workers, it alone will not help you retain talent for the long term.

Did you know that one of the reasons why top producers at some of the world's largest companies leave their role simply because they don't see themselves in the company's future? In other words, companies fail to

---

[2] Oswald, Andrew J., Proto, Eugenio and Sgroi, Daniel. (2015) *Happiness and Productivity*. Journal of Labor Economics, 33 (4). pp. 789-822.

show their key employees that they are valued and that their work is vital to the company's future.

You, on the other hand, will not allow that to happen. Ensure your key personnel have the resources and growth opportunities they desire. At the same continually communicate with them the mission and vision of the company and how they are a part of it.

Creating Careers

Taking a closer look at your team, there may be gaps missing or key roles that need to be filled. What we will be going through in this section is a simple way of creating a new job in your company and walking you through a streamlined hiring process you can adopt.

When crafting a new job role in the company, it's best to meet with the operations manager and department head that will be overseeing/managing the new hire and identify:

- The daily, weekly, and monthly task this role will perform
- What experiences the person performing this role should have had in order to succeed in this position
- Ideal DISC profile for the position
- Who this new hire will report to
- The vision of an ideal candidate that is in line with the company values and culture
- How this new job role plays a vital role in the company mission and vision
- What measurable goals will be in place and if there is an incentive to hit these goals
- Salary / compensation
- The level of access and tools this role needs in order to succeed
- The meetings this role will need to be a part of

Next, you need to decide if you will promote someone from within your company to fill this new role or if you will need to look externally to hire someone new.

Here's a streamlined hiring process that will allow you to easily fill this role if you don't have someone from within your company that you'd like to promote. If you already have a hiring and onboarding process in place, compare yours to this one below to ensure you aren't missing or overlooking something when you hire. I want to ensure you are bulletproof. This simple framework that can be adopted and improved to fit your organization.

Part 1: We're Hiring!

Post your job opening in:

- Your closed network
- Other people's networks (for example your mentor's network)
- Masterminds you are part of
- Your email list
- Open networks: LinkedIn, Job Boards

Make a note that your job posting should detail that you are looking for a long term person (you'll want to attract people who are ready to make a commitment).

Part 2: Gather Applications

Once you start getting responses and interest for the job, send them the application to get started. I like to send applications only to people who have expressed interest and have reached out to me after I make an announcement that I'm hiring.

Here is an application structure I use:

1- Capture Basic information
- Email
- Name

2 - Job-specific questions/experience related questions.
- You may ask the applicant to record a video detailing their work or a case study of results their work has created in the past (if applicable)
- Ask for references

3 - Goal-oriented questions

In this section of the application I am pre-framing applicants that I want to hire someone for the long term. At the same time however, I want to ensure they are a fit for the role TODAY and also 1 year from today.

Here are the types of questions that go in this section:
- Why are you applying for this role?
- What are your short term 1-year career goals?
- Where do you see yourself in 3 years? (Applications with short, non-descriptive answers will be disqualified)

4 - Confirmation that they understand they are applying for a long term position

In this final section, I like to have applicants read a confirmation statement that they are applying for a long term position. Again, I am framing their minds that I am both serious and have a long term opportunity for them.

Here is the statement I have applicants read and confirm:

Please read the following and type "I agree" below only if you agree with the following statement: "I am applying for a long term position and if I am considered for the opportunity I will put in the effort to succeed and grow in the company."

Part 3 Conduct Interviews

Once you have reviewed applications, reach out to serious applicants who have shown positive qualities in their application.

This is where your business specifics come into play. You can either have one or several interviews depending on the experience level of the role you are hiring for and your team size. If the role you are filling is not very complex, one simple interview will suffice.

Below is the interview flow I created and use for initial interviews and have made some of my best hires using it. Feel free to adapt it to your company.

The Interview Flow
1. Phase 1: Long Term Commitment Questions
    - *What to ask:* What are the skill sets you want to develop over the next 3 years?
    - *What to keep in mind:* Does our company match those skill sets? Are WE a good fit for them?

2. Phase 2: Set the company expectations/company culture and job expectations
    - *What to ask:* What does success look like to you in this role? Define success you are looking for in this role.
    - *What to keep in mind:* do they fit the expectations? Can they fill the needs of the company today? Do they have the potential to flourish in this role? How's their attitude?

3. Phase 3: Identify next steps

- Let them know what is going to happen next after the interview
  - Is HR going to call them, will you tell them they got the job on the spot, will they get an email a week later? Give the candidate closure.

If you are hiring for a more experienced position, I suggest you conduct a minimum of 2-3 interviews. The first will be a "get to know you" interview or phone call. You can use the same Interview Flow above.

The second interview however, should be with you and another team member or an all team meeting with the candidate. Your goal with this second interview is to see if the applicant fits your company culture and for you to get feedback from your team. Your team may pick up and see things you don't notice. Plus you want to protect your team culture by bringing in people who can easily adapt to your team.

If you are a sole business owner with no other team members or only have contracted vendors working for you, I suggest you ask a mentor or coach to be on this second call with you. Especially with high profile job roles, having a tight hiring process will save you from future headaches and problems that could have been avoided in this exact step.

By this point you should have a good idea whether or not this candidate has a place in your company. However, if you run a labor intensive business or your business depends on your team working cohesively, I highly recommend a third interview. This interview is more hands on and allows you to observe the candidate performing the work in a real world scenario or in a controlled environment.

After performing your interviews you will have a solid gauge if this candidate is a good fit for your company or not. Once you have decided on a new hire, continue with your new hire onboarding process.

Part 4 Onboarding New Team Member

Below is my sample onboarding process. You can adapt it to fit yours or cross reference the one you are currently using to ensure you don't miss a thing.

New Hire Onboarding
1. Set an official start date
2. Let them know they have the job!
3. Create a quarterly goal plan for the team member to have clear metrics and goals they need to hit
4. Send/receive the new hire contract/agreement
5. Get them the access they need
    1. Tools/logins
    2. Meeting invitations
6. Send a welcome email or package with the following:
    1. Welcome them to the team
    2. Send them trainings to get acquainted with your dashboards, team communication, and work environment
    3. Reaffirm start date
    4. Reaffirm meetings they will need to join
    5. Confirm their salary and run them through payroll/how to get paid
7. Get on an onboarding meeting on their first day of work to:
    1. Follow up on any training you sent them
    2. Personally walk them through getting acquainted with your company environment
    3. Walk them through the company office or software you use to communicate/collaborate with the team
    4. Let them know who they will be working with
    5. Answer any questions they have
    6. Direct them to any additional training/support for them to develop in their role and perform their work correctly

Autonomous Task Units

One of my favorite things as a business coach and consultant is to create leverage for CEOs and founders. This includes getting them out of the weeds of their company and creating autonomy within their team so the business can thrive without the constant dependence of the founder 24/7.

The biggest driver to this initiative is creating what I call *autonomous task units* within your company. Essentially we are taking your roles and connecting them together within the team to create mini teams for specific projects or initiatives in the company. This helps you, the owner, to do two key things properly:

1- **LEAD** the company more effectively
2- **FACILITATE SCALE** and the growth of your company

Ergo: **Expand Your Impact**

To do this, take out flashcards or sticky notes and "map" out your company by defining your key company actions (more on this in Chapter 7). Each key action gets its own flashcard or sticky note. Then add your team on their own sticky note and place them next to the specific actions tasks they own.

Next, review your key actions and personnel and see where there are overlaps, themes or connections. Consider what actions can be bundled up to create a process. Then, review what teams you can create that own those very specific parts of the process or the entire process as a whole. There is no one size fits all. Our goal with this exercise is to look at your business as a whole and try to create task units that can facilitate and own key processes in the company.

Having a team support you with your core business functions while you focus on planning, strategy, growth and impact, is one of the most liberating feelings my clients and I have in business.

My goal is for you to experience the same.

ACTION MAP

1. *Refine your termination policy and firing processes*
2. *Refine your hiring and onboarding process*
3. *Review your current team and assess if you have the team that will allow you to reach your horizons and drive the mission forward*
4. *Create autonomous task units by mapping out your company's key actions and personnel*

Chapter 6
Balancing Your CEO 80/20

The most important person you need to manage in your business is **yourself**.

As you come to understand and optimize each role in your company, it's now time to optimize your role as CEO. Our goal in this chapter is to work together to have a higher and better quality of life through simplifying your schedule, being intentional with your time, and being fully present at every moment in your day.

We will do that by balancing your 80/20.

If you don't know what 80/20 is, it is taken from the Pareto Principle which is a famous business management tool of measurement from Italian economist Vilfredo Pareto. In short, the principal states that approximately 80% of your outcomes and results stem from 20% of the input. How that translates over to your work is that a vast majority of the results that you're creating in your business right now are derived from very specific key actions. It is important to note that this principle is not always a clear cut 80/20. As a matter of fact, the exact number in your business does not matter. What does matter is you **knowing** what the "20%" actions are in your business. We want to identify and focus our efforts, resources, and energy in maximizing the "20%".

In order to do this, you must truly be working on CEO level tasks and also lead your team to focus the bulk of their energy and resources on their 20%. I created a simple exercise that we will do together in this chapter. It's a simple exercise that I give my clients in order to help them identify their 80/20.

Your CEO Map

We will start by having you map out your day from start to end for a week. I want you to identify what your routines are and what key actions you take daily, weekly, and monthly. When doing this exercise, I want you to identify actions that you love to do and areas in your business where you feel you are extraordinary at.

The next step is to review your map and highlight the tasks that are the biggest needle movers in your company. Next, I want you to circle actions that take you away from focusing on CEO level tasks. I don't believe in hard set rules of defining exactly what every CEO should be doing, however we can look at **areas of focus** CEOs *should* have in their company.

The following five areas are what I believe CEOs should focus on. The actual tasks and minute details surrounding each area can vary from business to business. This is an overall picture encompassing the areas CEOs should drive their attention and energy in their company:

CEO Focus Areas
- Company Vision
- Company Values
- Company Goals
- Maintaining Brand & Culture
- Business Development & Strategic Partnerships

Notice that these areas focus on high-level thinking and the future of the company. As a CEO your focus consists of communicating and sharing your company vision, maintaining company values, driving goal initiatives, and ensuring the right people are in place in order to meet those goals.

You must also have self awareness by knowing how your market perceives your brand and work to maintain a positive brand perception. As important as your consumer facing brand is, your internal team culture is arguably more important. Remember, your team is helping you achieve your goals and happier teams are more productive. I like to kid with my clients and tell them "who would have thought happiness is good for business?"

Lastly, you need to be focusing on developing strategic partnerships and relationships that will open new opportunities for the company. This isn't your typical business development role where you sell one-to-one. I want you to create relationships that open up one-to-one-to-**many** opportunities. These take *time* and a CEO.

As you reflect and review your own daily, weekly, and monthly actions and contrast them with what a CEO should be focusing on, you will begin to see some discrepancies. When you review your highlighted action items, do they fall in any of these areas? How about the action items you love to do or excel when you perform them?

What are you focusing on and what *should* you be focusing on?

Every action in your company is either done by you, someone else or a machine. For every other action item that is outside your 80/20, you need to make a decision:

- The items that you've circled and that do not have a place in your areas of focus, who in your company can you delegate these tasks to? If there is no current position to take those on, who can you hire?
- How about leveraging technology to take over some of these tasks?

This is where you begin to balance your 80/20. You may not have all the resources to hire or buy the greatest tech tools right now. However, you need to maintain a balance between what you need to do now, what you should be doing, and what you can hand off to other team members, consultants, contractors, administrative assistants or machines.

This is not an overnight process and there is building and training involved. Remember the train analogy? The fire of your company's train engine needs to keep going while at the same time you build tracks up ahead. We will dive more into building these tracks in Chapter 8.

Before you can say you've balanced your 80/20, we need to ensure you arrive to your day in an empowering way that encourages you to be present at every moment and progress through the day in natural flow state. We do this by taking a holistic approach to your day. Too many times as entrepreneurs we have the tendency to work 14-16 hours days and think that's alright. I understand that there are days where this is a must. No excuses. However, we are in this for the **long term**. I want you to maximize your business' success today and still have that momentum of success 20 years from now! I am not exaggerating. Success is not a one time thing. It's a journey. It's momentum. It's progress. So we need to ensure your days are set for long term success.

Remember the key habits we defined in your Goal Challenge in Chapter 3? We want to take these habits and also ensure you include self care, relationships, and what is important to you outside of business and set time aside to focus on these habits. This includes your 80/20 as well as all the daily tasks that pop up and last minute things you need to respond to.

You may begin to notice that we are now structuring and organizing your days and weeks... for some that can be scary.

I understand.

The thought of having too much discipline and too much structure can seem to ruin flexibility, creativity, and spontaneity...

Trust me, as a creative myself, I have been down that rabbit hole of perfectly structuring my day and only to have the master plan crumple when I spend too much time in one area or take longer than I planned for in another.

That's not what we are doing here.

I'd like to illustrate what I want us to accomplish here with a quick story of my first time visiting Kauai:

I was out in Kauai in January on a business trip. However, this business trip had Friday, Saturday, and Sunday open for exploration and personal time. So after the business meetings (essentially where we just strategized and planned the year with clients) we had leisure time to go and explore the island. Knowing this, I brought my wife and my brother on the trip. On our first day of exploration we didn't really have a set agenda of what we wanted to do, we just had ideas but nothing set in stone because that's what you're supposed to do on vacation, right?! Well, there were some unforeseeable events where a main road was closed so we spent roughly 2-3 hours trying to get out of traffic. From there since we didn't have a clear agenda, we made gut decisions of places we'd see for the rest of the day. And since it takes roughly 1-2 hours to drive to different parts of the island, we spent a majority of the time driving rather than sightseeing. In other words, the day was not optimized for leisure and sightseeing, which was our goal for the day. It was still a good day in my eyes but I can tell that we could have had a better outcome with a set plan. Getting back to our hotel room, without hesitation, we started creating a plan for the next day adding all our destination options and buffering extra time for added flexibility just in case we want to spend more time on one beach before we head to another part of the island. How well did our plan work out? Well, the difference in our experience the next day was like the difference between day and night. We were able to go to every spot that we wanted to visit, we had ample time spontaneity, and we were able to enjoy every moment. Driving back to our hotel room we felt pretty accomplished having done quite a bit that day.

What does this have to do with you?

When you're creating time blocks to add your habits into your day, it's important to plan out for variables and to buffer in time for spontaneity so at the end of the day you have an agenda that will allow you to move the needle every single day and also allow for 100% flexibility. I created these rules for myself after roughly 8 years of refining my personal approach to my schedule because as a creative, if I'm extremely regimented without flexibility, life can feel monotone. And to restate the fact that with a super regimented schedule, if you miss one appointment or spend too much time in another, you ultimately create unnecessary stress in your day. And yes I can attest that even with running a company, you can plan for flexibility and spontaneity.

As you figure out what your time blocks are I encourage you to create a realistic approach to your day but also ensure you are diligent to have distraction free working blocks (especially in your 80/20 activities). I'd go as far as suggesting you to plan your 80/20 activities first thing in your day and completing your day's most important actions before you ever open up your email or answer other people's requests for the day. This will allow you to drive the impact of your company and be in a better mental and business state to answer the demands of the day.

With anything, there are days where things don't always go as planned. Every day is different and if you miss something one day, you can make up for it the next. Remember, we are focusing on the long-term game. Now, don't take this as slack to then create bad habits. Stick to the plan and adjust as needed. Your key metric here is progress.

Action *x* Consistency = Progress

This is how you're going to win.

Lastly, I encourage you to look at your time blocks like puzzle pieces that you can stack in different order and rearrange depending on what season in life you're in. You can test different settings as you find a sequence of time blocks that fit best for you at this current time in your life and in your business. I do recommend you stick to a new plan for at least 1 to 2 weeks to ensure you've given yourself enough time to adjust. If you ever feel frustrated with your daily actions or lack thereof, it could be that your day is out of sequence. Remember, be flexible and rearrange your time blocks in any way you see fit.

Below is an example of my current time blocks but so you don't feel overwhelmed or some sort of pressure to mimic what I do, I set my blocks in sequence of my key habits. I will set the times I wake and sleep to give you context. Please remember, this is just a simple snapshot of how I live my life and how I prioritize my time blocks in order to live the lifestyle I want as well as provide the most value that I can to my clients:

4:30 Wake
- Prayer
- Exercise & Studying
- Prayer
- Planning
- Creating & Connecting
- Coaching & Consulting
- Studying
- Family / Friends

9:30 Sleep

ACTION MAP

Balancing Your 80/20

Are you investing your focus and energy like the CEO your company needs you to be? Let's ensure you're 100% focused on the mission and important aspects of your life.

Step 1: Day Mapping
1. Outline your current day and week on a piece of paper or sticky notes. Review the following questions:
    - What are your routines?
    - What key actions do you love doing?
    - Where do you shine in your business (what are you extraordinary at)?
    - What are the key actions your business requires?
2. Highlight the key 80/20 actions you take.
3. Circle actions that take you away from focusing on CEO level tasks.
4. Compare your actions to the CEO Focus Areas:
    - Company Vision
    - Company Values
    - Company Goals
    - Maintaining Brand & Culture
    - Business Development & Strategic Partnerships

Step 2: Balancing Your 80/20
Looking at the actions you circled, decide:
- Can you delegate these actions to someone on your team? What training do they need?
- Do you need to hire someone to delegate these actions to? If so, who?
- Can you utilize technology to complete these actions? What do you need to build or get built for you?

Step 3: Building Your Time Blocks

1. *Review your key habits from Chapter 3*
2. *Review your calendar and schedule your key habits and 80/20 actions*
3. *Set enough time to allow for flexibility and include what's important in your life on your calendar*

Use this space to brainstorm different time block ideas.

Chapter 7
Reducing Waste and Maximizing Your Company's Actions

As you go through the exercises in this book, since one of our core focuses is to maximize the highest leverage activities in your business, you may have noticed inefficiencies, weaknesses, and flaws in your current company's infrastructure start to surface. In this chapter we're going to roll up our sleeves and dive deep into pinpointing the exact efficiencies and their root causes. In doing so we may also discover opportunities that we can leverage so you can expand your impact even further.

Your Core 3

What we're going to do now is break down your business and your business model into very succinct parts. Your business has three core departments. Those three departments are operations, marketing, and product/service fulfillment. It's very simple and this is how simple business should be.

Let's define this further so you understand what key actions occur under every department.

Your operations departments focuses on:
- Strategic Planning
- Business Plan Strategy
- Administrative Tasks
- Human Resources
    - Recruiting

- Hiring
- Firing
- Training
- Developing Job Roles & Careers
- Performance Reviews
- Team Building
• Financials
  - Accounting
  - Budgeting
  - Forecasting
  - Payroll
  - Profit & Loss Statements

Your marketing department focuses on:
- Customer Acquisition
- Branding
- Messaging
- Sales Team
- Customer Journey

Your product department focuses on:
- Client Onboarding and Offboarding
- Product/Service Fulfillment
- Product/Client Management

One of the beautiful things about seeing your company in these three core departments is that you can see how your company actions seamlessly work together from a holistic point of view. For example, your marketing message is your prospective customers first experience with your brand and as customers progress further down the customer journey you've created they'll interact with different aspects of your brand: from your sales and marketing department to your onboarding, fulfillment, customer retention, and client management department. What your customers won't see is the magic that is happening in the background. What's silently ensuring everything in your company is working properly is your company's operations.

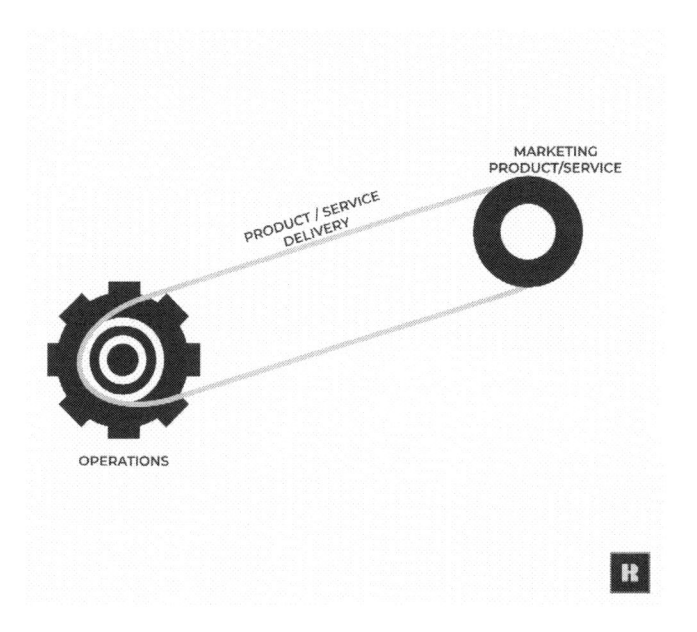

I see most creative entrepreneurs solely focused on their marketing and perhaps some on the fulfillment side of their business. But what is most often missed is how intricate their operations are and how they play a larger role to the success and growth of their business.

Breaking it down to a simple math formula: your product or service is a numeral, your marketing is the multiplier, and your operations is the exponent.

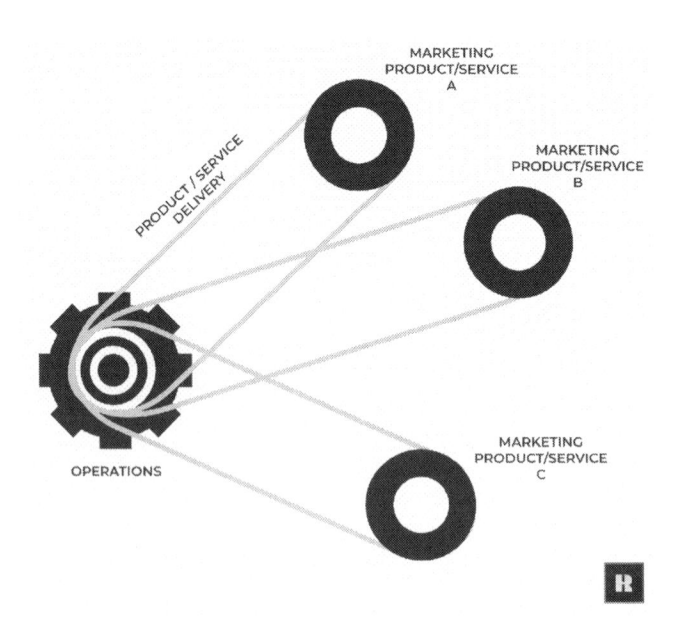

As you grow your company, if you don't have proper operations to support your growth, the business will just crumble. This is why we focus on building a solid foundation in your business that will allow you to dictate the growth of your company.

Now that we've detailed the three core departments of your business, let's find ways to improve each. Let's break down your current three departments and identify the key actions you perform in each (I hope you're starting to see a trend here). Remember, these key actions are done by you, someone on your team or a machine.

As you mapped out your actions in the previous chapter, are your team's current actions aligned with the company's 80/20 and in line to support the company mission? Take the time to meet with your executive team or set a meeting with yourself and review every aspect and personnel in your company and see if their main focuses and actions are directed towards their 80/20 actions. You may have some eye-opening results and see that your team's time is not being allocated to priorities as it should be and resources are spent in the wrong areas.

As you spend time reviewing your company and team, as the leader you must take complete ownership of the inefficiencies that are happening. This is part of the process and ultimately what you signed up for when you decided to run a company. Ask yourself what you could have done to prevent this from happening and what you will do to ensure leaks are fixed. This is the first step to allow you to ensure success across the board. On the flip side, we also want to congratulate you for the positive momentum and correct things you are doing in the company. These successes are your fault as well and what we want to do is package and refine them to duplicate your success in less time. The key actions in this stage are patching up flat tires in your company and maximizing the good that's happening.

Now as you may notice, you will come across a lot of semi good things your company is doing. All they need are minor tweaks in order to be excellent. As you review these, you want to take account of every one of them and identify how else they may add value to your company or the marketplace.

For example, perhaps your team is collecting information in the form of experience through their client interactions and this information is not being broken down to derive key takeaways that can be applied in other areas of the business or with other clients. It first takes 1) awareness that this isn't being done and 2) action to solve the problem through connection and communication.

In another example, what if you find opportunities to add more value to the marketplace and increase your impact by repurposing information, experience, or company assets and creating new products and services? This is actually my story when I found myself supporting and helping highly successful companies grow and thrive. My mentor John Morgan prompted me to be aware of the key actions I was taking that helped these businesses succeed and over the years I studied and refined my own process, which led to where I am today.

Your next steps here are to identify the 80/20 within your company's core departments and begin to get a better grasp of what you do differently and better in your business.

Then, if you want, ponder on new ideas that can drive either new developments for your company internally or new offerings for the marketplace. Don't get overwhelmed on the how just yet.

In the next chapter, we will go over how to package and refine your successes so your business and impact can live beyond your efforts.

ACTION MAP

1. *Breakdown your company's key action within your 3 core departments*
    - *Operations*

    - *Marketing*

    - *Product/Service*

2. *Identify if your team's actions are aligned with the 80/20 key actions within each department.*
    - *For inefficiencies, review what could you have done to prevent this from happening and make a plan to eliminate this from ever happening in the future.*

3. *Highlight the good that is currently happening in your company and look at it through two different perspectives:*
    - *How might you reutilize this positive action/outcome in other areas of your business? How can this add more value to your team?*

    - *How might you package these positive key actions/outcomes and create new offerings in the marketplace to new or existing customers?*

Chapter 8
Designing Your Evergreen Flows

Now we come to the core building block of the book where we apply every concept we've learned thus far in order to create truly autonomous workflows, or what I call *Evergreen Flows*. Evergreen because they contain your essential business actions and solidify them into a repeatable process that can be improved over time and repetition. For some, this means having your business work **without you** as you hand it off to another CEO and team while you grow other businesses or opportunities to expand your impact. For most, however, this means having your business work autonomously **with you** so you can focus on driving your mission forward without overwhelm while beating competitors with superior quality, serving more clients, growing your revenue, and expanding your impact.

These next two chapters are built to help you succeed in regardless of which track you decide to take in your business. But before we go further, we need to discuss how Evergreen Flows play a vital part of a much, much bigger ecosystem we are building here for your business.

Evergreen Flows are a communication tool that allow you to blueprint and package your key company habits for repeatable scale, with the goal to help you maintain quality, precision and increase excellence over time. They are simple by nature yet flexible as they evolve and are refined by your team as you scale. This is how world class companies design excellence into their DNA.

In short, Evergreen Flows are the key that will allow you to eliminate bottlenecks in your business. There is a reason why we are discussing this deep into the book. I could have started the book with Evergreen Flows; however, that would have been a disservice to you since we have to build the foundational building blocks we went over in previous chapters first. Having those foundational blocks not only puts you ahead of most businesses I've come across, they also will perfectly foster and increase the effectiveness of the Evergreen Flows we will build for your business. Your team will be able to seamlessly adapt them and your leadership team will have a solid pulse to ensure they are used, maintained, and improved over the lifetime of your company.

That's my goal for you.

However, there is a very strategic way you have to implement Evergreen Flows in your company and ensure they are refined over time. That's why I have dedicated the entire next chapter to help you implement these flows into your company and lay out the action items and areas that need your focus so you can be a facilitator of your company's scale.

What Is An Evergreen Flow?

Coming to age in the digital world, all the work I have done in helping train hundreds of entrepreneurs across the globe, mentoring, coaching, and working with companies to facilitate their scale, has been done in my home office in San Diego. I've started a business with a friend whom I never met in person and have helped double million dollar team across 7 different time zones, all remote.

The beauty of remote teams is that a lot of work can get done in a very short amount of time. There's less distraction and more time to be able to be in "the zone" when you work. However, one of the biggest drawbacks to remote work is the fact that communication gaps exist and miscommunications can happen all too frequently. This is the Achilles' heel of remote teams.

Regardless if you are a remote or in-person team, does this sound familiar:

- You constantly roll up your sleeves to take on the work yourself because your team is "not doing it right"
- You constantly answer the same questions and repeat the same instructions
- You and your team are paralyzed by overwhelm and lack of direction when undertaking big projects (internally or for clients)
- You want to focus on just creating content and sales but are stuck "doing" most of the busy day-to-day work
- You can't guarantee the quality of your team's work because you don't know exactly how they do what they do
- You can't easily replicate results
- You have become the disgruntled employee in your own business
- You feel like you're not making traction and frequently find yourself feeling frustrated…

As mentioned in Chapter 2, my goal is to find ways to **lessen the gap between information and action**. To combat the issues I was seeing with the companies I was helping, I created a communication tool that allowed teams to easily understand the work at hand, see how their role plays part of a bigger part of the company, and easily grasp the action items they needed to take *in substantially less time*. I'm talking 5-15 minutes, tops. Clear action can be taken, teams stop asking the same questions twice, and leadership teams can spend more time driving the company mission forward.

Done right, implementing Evergreen Flows in your company will allow you to:
- Have peace of mind
- Duplicate success in less time
- Get the best out of your team (not just the most work but high quality work)
- Increase salability (if you ever want to sell your business)

...and ultimately **create a greater impact.**

That's what I help my clients do and that's exactly what I want to do for you.

I created Evergreen Flows to be designed around your impact so you can strategically hone in your resources and energy on your key company habits that allow you to increase your impact. I also incorporated the big three learning modalities, visual, auditory, and written (known as tactical learning), to ensure clarity across diverse teams.

Remember the Core 3 departments in your business and their 80/20 actions? These are where your key company habits live. These are the revenue drivers, bottom line needle movers and actions that help increase your company's impact. By solidifying them into your company's DNA with Evergreen Flows, you'll be able to scale your communication, scale your team, and scale your impact.

Here is a sample:

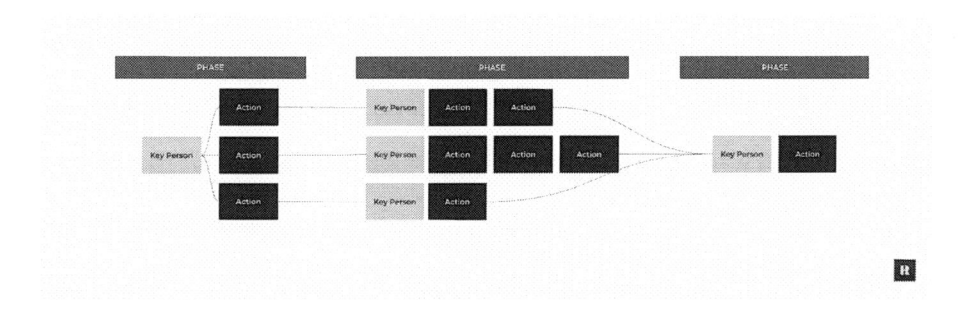

The key to Evergreen Flows' success is its ease of creation and implementation. They start out as simple maps that outline the very key habits of your company and break them down into a series of phases, action items and deliverables that are assigned and detailed to the respective team members. From there, Evergreen Flows are documented with detailed, clear written instructions and topped off with an audiovisual overview. And since Evergreen Flows are an essential building block to your company's success, they don't take hours to develop. You could get your entire company or department mapped out and detailed over a weekend, depending on your company size. And since this is a creative process, designing and creating Evergreen Flows is fun. Even if you don't think it's fun, you'll definitely enjoy the fact that you're eliminating bottlenecks in your business which is both wonderful to think about and enjoyable when you experience it.

We also build Evergreen Flows with the future in mind. Due to their flexibility you can create them once, have the team adopt them and have the team refine and nurture their evolution **on their own**. You'll also be able to identify bottlenecks and potential problems before they ever arise because you are getting a clear picture of every aspect of your company.

Enough talking about them.

Let's Build Your First Evergreen Flow

As we begin, we will need to get essential tools ready. All you'll need here are thick markers, sticky notes, and butcher paper or a whiteboard. You'll notice we aren't going digital first. We want to allow creativity to flow and connect your brain with your hands as we begin the design process. You're all set to start.

Phase 1: Creativity On Demand
Being a creative process, the first step is to get your creative juices running.

Anyone can be creative.

I like to think of creativity as a muscle and like a muscle, we want to activate it consciously. In order to harness your creativity on demand we want to get you in "the zone" by getting you to move around and be in a positive headspace. You can do this through listening to music that you enjoy and going outside for a walk while getting some sunlight. Listening to any pleasurable music will give you a boost in cognition for about 15 minutes[3]. Once you get yourself focused and in a creative flow, move to Phase 2.

Phase 2: Mapping

Pick what key habit you want to create an Evergreen Flow for from your Core 3 departments: Operations, Marketing, and Product/Service.

Most client's don't know where to start. We typically do a deep dive session to identify the key habits they need to build Evergreen Flows for first. Remember: your company habits are just a series of actions done by you, someone on your team, or a machine.

Here are a few examples:

If you are focusing in your operations department, perhaps you are building an Evergreen Flow for your hiring and new team member onboarding. For your marketing department, maybe you are building a flow for your prospecting and sales process or you're designing a flow for your content creation and syndication plan. If you're dialing in your product delivery or service fulfillment department, perhaps you're creating a seamless onboarding experience for your new clients or designing a flow to strengthen your customer support and retention habits.

---

[3] Medina, John. Brain Rules (Updated and Expanded): *12 Principles for Surviving and Thriving at Work, Home, and School*. Pear Press, 2014.

Start with the flow that your company needs right now.

If everything is a priority, then nothing is a priority.

Using your sticky notes, look at the key habit you're creating the flow for and write down each action on its own sticky note. If you have multi-colored sticky notes, I highly suggest using the same color for your key actions.

When doing this exercise, you want to be sure you're using a THICK marker, not a thin pen. I learned this from IDEO design thinking. The thicker your marker is, the harder it is to add details on a small sticky note. The thinner the pen is the easier and more tempting it is to write down details and sub-tasks within each action item. Don't do that!

As you are overlooking all the actions that make up your habit, identify how you can move around action items or group actions together in order to create a series of phases in which these actions occur.

Here we are breaking down the habits into small components in order to harness control and create clarity within your key habit. The number of phases in a habit vary, however, I like to follow what is found to be beautiful in nature and art and apply it to business by using the Fibonacci Sequence (0, 1, 1, 2, 3, 5, 8, 13, 21, 34, …). Therefore, I like to assign 1, 2 or 3 phases in a key habit. Once you have the actions in a series of phases that make logical sense to you and you feel good about, label each phase using the sticky notes. Simply label them Phase 1, Phase 2 and so on. If you have different colored stickies, use a different color to identify your phases.

Next, you want to identify the *key people* you need in every phase of the key habit you are designing for. Do you need different roles at different phases? Or can one person own the entire habit? As you distinguish and identify the key people that are needed to successfully execute the company habit, write their name and role down on a separate sticky note. Use a different colored sticky here if possible.

Phase 3: Streamline

Now that you have taken your key company habit and have identified every action, have combined those actions into a series of phases, and have identified the key people you need to successfully execute the key company habit, it's time to take a step back and then come back with a fresh mind to connect the dots. Take a 5-minute break, 15 tops. This is not a siesta.

Grab a water, go outside, and relax your mind for a bit because this is where we are streamlining your key habits and eliminating bottlenecks.

When you come back from your break, you should be looking at a 10,000 ft. overview of your first draft Evergreen Flow. This is why we wrote everything in thick marker, so you could have a holistic overview of the entire flow, start to finish, without worrying about the details.

As you review your flow you want to walk through the key phases and actions in your head, go through them logically and imagine every step of the process. Your first goal is to identify any breaks in the flow or any way you could make the actions flow more seamlessly and naturally, adapted to how your company and team work.

You also want to keep a sharp eye on the actions that are being done and ask if an action or series of actions can be done by a machine through automation. Circle these areas and research tools that can help automate these steps. I get asked frequently what tools business owners should use and to be frank, that's a useless question because every business has it's unique way of operating. I always answer by saying "it's not the tools that matter, it's *how* you use them". After going through this exercise, you can see why I answer in that way. As you identify the actions that you can potentially automate, ask the better question "how do I streamline and automate X, Y, and Z actions for my ABC flow?". Now, you can ask me or do a little bit of research what tools exist that can help you automate those actions. The decision of which tool to use now comes down to preference and that one that will be easily adapted and used by your team. Remember: we only buy the tools we *need* and *will use*.

When you've refined the flow by removing, adding or moving around action items and/or phases, your next goal is to identify potential areas of *drop-off in communication*.

Are there areas where information or tasks are passed to another person?

Are there areas where key information is needed?

Are there areas that you know your team has gotten stuck in the past?

You want to leave no stone unturned and find every possible error that could occur in your flow.

As you go through this, you will also clearly see areas in your flow where bottlenecks exist.

Are there key actions that are being held up at a certain point or by a certain person? Here is your chance to completely obliterate overwhelm and eliminate bottlenecks by anticipating needs.

It's time to take out your fine-tuned pen.

With the drop-off in communication and bottlenecks clearly identified, list out the resources and answers to the key questions that came up in these flow disrupt areas. The resources you can provide are checklists on how to complete action items, templates that you can create or have your team create to allow action items to be completed faster with clarity, access to key tools that will allow your team to work more effectively or "if-then" scenarios to empower your team to have outlined recourse actions when needed and be able to make decisions on their own given by your framework.

A key thing to keep in mind here is that you can **never assume**. Never assume your team knows where to get the resources, or know exactly what to do. That's allowing yourself to be a bottleneck because perhaps it's clear knowledge for you to know where to get the resources or how to do something, but for the team it may not be as clear.

Phase 4: Feedback Loops

Your Evergreen Flow version 1.0 does not have to be pretty. In fact, it does not have to be perfect. It just has to be to the point where someone else in your team can see it and understand it.

In this phase, you will meet with the following team members for 15 minutes to overview the flow with them and get their feedback and ensure it's 110% clear.

Meet with the following people:

- The key people who are actively involved in executing the key company habit and are named in the flow
- The manager who oversees the specific company department you are creating the flow for
- Your leadership team and/or operations manager

When discussing with your team, you want to present the flow of actions and have your team follow the same exercises you did in Phase 3. Does it make logical sense? Do they see any drop-off or bottlenecks you didn't? Do they have questions you didn't consider or ask for resources that you didn't add or scenarios you didn't think of? Since you already did most of the heavy lifting by designing and creating the flow, it will only take a small amount of work to integrate their feedback into the flow.

It is critical that you **do not skip this step**. I once created an Evergreen Flow for a content marketing creation and syndication plan and met with the CEO to discuss the flow as detailed above. In less than 10 minutes we were able to shift about 10% of the work to the front end of the flow and added a template to replace some of the action items in the flow. This allowed us to reduce the time content went from the "create" phase to the "published" phase. Since content marketing helped drive revenue for this business, by reducing the time it took a content piece to reach the market, we increased the frequency and opportunities the business had to make a profit.

Even if you are a solopreneur, it is still important that you ensure the Evergreen Flow makes sense to you, that you like it, and that you can see yourself utilizing it in your work. If you have a business coach, mentor, or support group, go over the flow with them to get feedback that can strengthen your workflow.

Phase 5: Going Live With A One Page S.O.P.

Now that you have your Evergreen Flow refined and ready to go live we want to transfer it over to digital. You can do this in several ways. You can simply take a photo of it and ensure that the details are clearly read. Or you can use a tool to clean up and create the flow digitally. You can use any tool that allows you to draw or map out flows. I personally like to use Google Drawings since it's free and accessible to nearly anyone. However, as noted above, use the tool that suits your preference and that your company can easily adapt.

Once we have the Evergreen Flow in digital form, it's time to document it into what I call a **One Page S.O.P.** (which stands for standard operating procedure). The reason why we only use one page is to not overwhelm the team reading it and to reduce the time between information and action.

Here is the outline of the One Page S.O.P. that will allow you to clearly communicate with your team what and how to perform key company habits and also allow your team to evolve the Evergreen Flow on their own:

Tile: Department That Holds The Key Company Habit (OPS, MKTG, PROD) - Name Of The Key Habit

i.e. PROD - New Client Onboarding

Purpose:
Define the Outcome/what will this key habit looks like when done

Ownership:
List out anyone on the team who is involved with the flow and distinguish who will own and be responsible for overseeing the successful completion of this company habit and maintain the Evergreen Workflow up to date.

- Owner: {ROLE TITLE} - {TEAM MEMBER'S NAME}
- {ROLE TITLE} - {TEAM MEMBER'S NAME}
- {ROLE TITLE} - {TEAM MEMBER'S NAME}
- {ROLE TITLE} - {TEAM MEMBER'S NAME}
- {ROLE TITLE} - {TEAM MEMBER'S NAME}

Last Updated On:
When has this Evergreen Flow last been updated and have we come up with a better way of doing this? Is this the most efficient way to perform this flow? Should we update this?

Evergreen Flow

Link out to an editable digital document or tool where the owner of the flow can edit and make improvements as needed. Also include an image of the up to date flow here so the team can visually see all phases and action items at once.

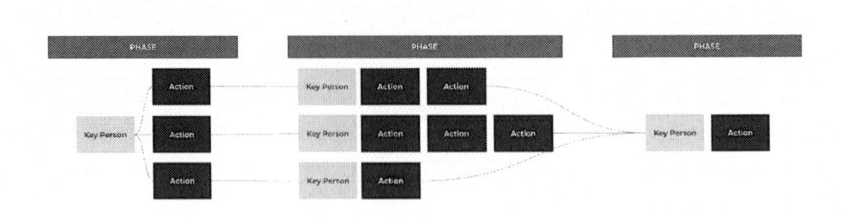

Video Overview

For those on your team that are more visual and auditory learners, create a screen recording video to detail the flow from start to finish. In the video, outline the action items and phases in the flow and show the available resources the team has access to in order to complete the company habit successfully.

Resources

List out and give access (links and logins) to the resources your team will need to complete this habit. Having it here in one place allows for ease of access and ensures your team is equipped to succeed. You also want to detail any "if-then" scenarios so your team who handles this company habit can have a clear framework of what action items to take when the unexpected happens.
- Checklists
- Templates
- Logins / Access / Links / Tools
- If-Then Scenarios

Expectations

In this final section of the One Page S.O.P. you want to add details of how long this key company habit takes to perform or how long each phase takes to execute. This will allow the owner or manager of the department to easily monitor and manage the team. It will also allow you to see if future improvements to the Evergreen Flow or addition of new resources will allow the team to work more efficiently or cut down costs.

Lastly, you also want to note how often this habit and flow will be executed. Is your team expected to perform this daily, weekly, bi-weekly, monthly? Remember: leave no stone unturned.
- Frequency: i.e. 1x/ week, daily,
- ETA for completion of {the Key Company Habit Name}:
- ETA for Phase 1 completion:

Immediate Implementation

As you begin to create your Evergreen Flows you will find that some flows can be immediately implemented into your company through the technology you are currently using. For example, say your business uses software to facilitate new client onboarding or cloud based tools that help automate every key task within a workflow. You may be able to implement what you designed almost immediately by editing the sequences and settings in the tools you currently use. You should still meet with your team before making any changes. However, the feedback loops and changes can take place instantaneously after approval and review with the team.

Continue to document these Evergreen Flows as noted in the previous sections in order to ensure your entire team understands how these flows work and so you can delegate ownership of the flow to the proper team member.

Bonus Phase:
Leveraging Evergreen Flows To Multiply Opportunity And Increase Your Impact

Being able to easily communicate key business habits across your internal team is essential to allow you to scale your communications and team. In the same way, being able to clearly communicate value or information to the external marketplace allows you to increase perceived value, sales, and open new opportunities to package and sell your company's knowledge.

As discussed in Chapter 7, you can leverage what your company excels at to create opportunities within the company or on the marketplace. Let's say you have a unique way of solving a problem that isn't a trade secret and others in your market may find valuable. Because you've been able to map your unique methodology using Evergreen Flows and can clearly communicate it to others, you can package your unique methodology into a new product or service. In another example, say your company through the refined Evergreen Flows you've created is able to develop new market intelligence in a shorter amount of time. Such information is valuable for your company to outperform your competition and for your team to be able to do their work more strategically and intelligently.

Clear communication is how good ideas can be shared. Both internally within your company and externally to the marketplace. There is a tremendous amount of opportunity that Evergreen Flows can create in your company that help you increase your impact and drive your mission forward.

ACTION MAP

Create your first Evergreen Flow by following the exercises in this chapter and put together your first One Page S.O.P. following the outline in Phase 5.

Repeat this for every key habit in your company that you want to have operate autonomously without you or with your limited involvement while you focus on your 80/20 actions.

Chapter 9
Scaling Your Impact Through Heroic Leadership

The two keys to successfully facilitating growth in your company are clear *communication* and *autonomy*. By adding clarity to your team, everyone will be on the same page and work in unison towards success. By empowering your team to have the access and resources needed to execute their roles allows you to eliminate the bottlenecks in your business. Keep in mind that siloed communications are parasites that cause waste and confusion within companies. And lack of communication causes assumptions which in turn cause errors. We will not be having neither in your company.

Any company can implement clear communication and autonomy. However, what will allow you to leave a legacy by creating a real impact, separate your company from the crowd, and truly build a thriving culture where people want to work with you is to tie clear communications and autonomy with *heroic leadership*. As the old saying goes: "it's not what you do that matters but *how* you do it."

The topic of leadership is boundless and I am not going to cover every nook and cranny in this chapter. Rather, I am going to outline 5 essential areas that you will need to focus on as a heroic leader as you scale your company. We will apply these 5 areas to clear communication and autonomy so you can see how everything we've gone through in this book connects and can be integrated within your company.

Imagine you and your team working holistically, with transparent communication across teams, tracking towards finishing deadlines on time. Everyone knows what to do and how to do it, utilizing their resources and teammates effectively and efficiently. You as the leader, facilitating their movement and having a clear gauge of progress and results as you drive the growth of the company and expand your impact. This is what we have been working towards and this is my goal for you.

Remember, business is *simple*.

Why *Heroic*?

There are many distinctions we can make that separate managers from leaders. However, the distinction I want to make is between leaders who lead and leaders who *inspire*.

Heroic leadership begins with taking on and facing responsibility, never shying away from it. It comes with a dedication to the mission, the people involved in achieving the mission, and taking action on whatever path leads to the greatest good towards success. Heroic leaders firmly know they own the outcomes produced by themselves and their team, both positive and negative. Giving credit to the team when accomplishing feats and not blaming others when errors or mistakes happen. Heroic leaders know that they can delegate any task in the company but can never delegate the responsibility. There is wisdom in knowing the difference.

By understanding the essence of a heroic leader, you can and will become one through focus and repetition of actions that drive heroic leadership. Not only will you achieve your mission and Called-To goals in a virtuous manner, but most importantly, you will inspire those around as you progress on your journey, even those whom you did not intend to or thought you would inspire.

The 5 Essential Focus Areas

Going Through Growing Pains

Just as you undertake any trek, you want to know what lays ahead. To be realistic. To know what to expect and how to best prepare. As you grow your company and scale your team, growing pains will happen. Remember our analogy of the train? Part of the growth pains are building the train tracks while at the same time fueling the engine. Depending on the speed of your growth and how well you have gone through all exercises in this book, growing pains may go smoothly or be a bit rough.

The one thing you as a heroic leader must possess when going through growing pains is patience and most importantly, *patience with yourself*. You must have patience with your team, never losing your temper nor losing hope and maintain the course. Being firm in your direction and fearless in the face of the high stresses that can occur when going through growth pains will empower your team to hold fast alongside you. No matter what your growth or scale goals are, growing pains are part of the process.

As you read this, it may come across that we are focusing on the negative part of scaling your company... looking at a rough road ahead and the unflattering side of business. That couldn't be further from the truth. As a heroic leader we must face reality as it is and act proactively to pave the path in which we will lead our teams through. We are not settling nor accepting excuses. Scaling your company will expose the weakness in your planning and company infrastructure. The faster you grow, the faster these weaknesses will be exposed. Yet there is a stark difference between accepting your weaknesses as a limit and knowing that you have a weakness.

When I first began training for my endurance obstacle course races my training was sporadic. I would focus on cardiovascular exercises maybe once a week and the rest focus on powerlifting to get into better shape. I could hardly maintain running past 5 miles and enduring 2 hour workouts without excessive breaks. I remember running the half-marathon in Carlsbad, California one January day and my right quadricep failed me by locking up around mile 7. I could hardly walk. When I did finish the race, I knew that whatever event I had coming next I had to ensure I trained more frequently and to the point where I would push past my physical and mental weaknesses every time. Nearly a year later, having done two 8-10 mile obstacle course races and maintained the habit of pushing through limits in my training, I've been able to run 10 miles on any given weekend (one month we did that twice), endure 2-3 hour workouts with less stopping and train for 12 hour+ obstacle races. What would have become of me if I had accepted my weakness as a limit?

There will be a point in your company's growth that you will encourage and even set up stress tests of your own! This is not to shoot yourself in the foot, but rather to continually refine and eliminate any weakness in your company. There are many ways to conduct a stress test since every business is unique, I would need to come and customize one for you. However, one of the easiest ways for you to conduct your own stress test, is for you or a key leader in your company to take a week's vacation. Can you as a leader let go? Can you trust the workflows and team you put in place? Have you trained your team well enough to work without you? Have you set them up for success to work autonomously?

With repetition, over time, of refining and eliminating weaknesses in your company, you will find that the growing pains will subside. They may also arise stronger with any major changes in your company. Regardless, if they arise, you know they are part of the process and that you have the power to push through them.

Setting The Stage

Your team will learn from you in two ways: what you say and how you behave. You set the stage. As a heroic leader, it is critical you take into heavy consideration every word you say and how you foster your relationships with your team members. Even if you are a team of one, I highly encourage you to put into practice these disciplines because as the saying goes: *how you practice is how you play*.

Believe it or not your team is listening to every word you say especially when it pertains to their welfare. I learned this early on in my career as a young leader, not knowing the weight of my own words. The more I saw how my words affected the teams I led, even the slightest tone or phrase, the more I began to work on improving myself to truly live up to the enormous responsibility of taking care of a team. You must do the same. Every word you say matters. How you talk about others outside the company and about other team members, matters. How you respond to high pressure situations or stressors, matters.

As a heroic leader you must keep your cool in the face of storms and, most importantly, know the ounce of every letter, of every word, of every sentence you say and write. If you do not take this seriously for the sake of your team and the mission of your company, no one will take you seriously and you will lose trust.

Your team will also learn from you by osmosis. By the way you act and behave around your team you are setting an unsaid standard of how they should act and behave. A heroic leader acts and behaves as the title states: heroic. That means you must care for your team unlike other shoddy leaders. They will come to know the difference, either coming to work with you from other companies with weak leadership or moving to another company. You do this by maintaining a positive and healthy working relationship with every one of your team members. Not only team members but I also encourage key vendors, suppliers, contractors and the like. Reason being is that other companies treat their outside vendors and contractors simply as they are, vendors and contractors. Going the extra mile does not only reinforce a positive habit but will also teach others on your team how you do business.

A heroic leader teaches as much by word as by doing. It is not necessary needed to be done all the time, but being in the trenches with your team does light a spark within them. It also allows you to see the true needs of the team versus their wants, allowing you to gauge a more accurate pulse of where your team stands in regard to the culture, relationship, and resources needed to succeed. It does not matter how you see yourself as a leader, but how your team sees you. Developing these insights and relationships with your team is essential to effectively leading your team to success.

Executing Tough Decisions

When you're moving fast and working to scale your company, your mind may be in a thousand places. Making difficult decisions is the crux of any leadership team but making the right one, the one that has the greatest benefit to all, is of heroic leaders.

The two things I suggest when making tough decisions while growing your company are to make data driven decisions when possible and ensure you have enough feedback loops to support your decision. As discussed in Chapter 2, it is essential to track the core metrics of your company in order to gauge its pulse. Now, there may be some decisions that will require data outside of your core metrics. It is important to know that whatever question you ask in your company, especially when making tough decisions, to then look for the data within your company that will allow you to make the best choice. Some data will be qualitative, especially when working with and managing people. For example, if you are deciding whether or not to keep an employee you may look at their work output to gauge performance but also look at the soft skills such as their attitude towards their work and team. Such decisions are not as simple as that but this at least gives you a simple guide on how to accurately diagnose and make proper recommendations when facing difficult situations.

After you've gotten the data associated with the decision at hand, the next step is to get enough feedback from key players that will allow you to confirm the right decision. I call this a sanity check. It is important to keep in mind that I am not proposing you marinate a decision for longer than needed. We are also not looking to make rash or impulsive decisions either. As heroic leaders we must take all factors into consideration, looking at the cold hard facts of the numbers, being able to understand the story behind them, and having trusted team members to help you cross reference your thinking. Even if you are a mighty team of one you should still have a mentor, coach, or group of advisors of which you can get the needed feedback from. It is always best to get the educated opinion from someone who isn't buried deep with the problem of your business.

Fueling Others

Great leaders lead teams. Heroic leaders lead *and* create leaders.

When we worked on designing your Evergreen Flows to communicate key habits and actions to your team, we were working to reduce the gap between information and action. But what if we could remove that gap entirely and our team could think as we did? This isn't to say that your way of thinking is perfect, however, what if we could empower your team to arrive at the same or better solution as you can? You can do this by nurturing future leaders in your company on how to think through *decision delegation* where you empower and train your team over time to make their own decisions when appropriate. One simple way of doing this is to mandate that if anyone on your team comes to you with a question, they must always have with them 2-3 possible solutions or recommendations. There are times where the question at hand is a bit more complex, but for the majority of questions you receive as a leader, your team can help provide their own recommendations.

This exercise over time allows you to do two things:

1. Be able to train your team on how you make decisions so they can execute decisions on their own where appropriate.
2. Allow you as the leader to see where your team lacks in training or clarity.

"I know what you are going to say" or "I knew you were going to say that" are key phrases you'll hear that indicate you are on the right track. It may take a few months and regular feedback to arrive at this, however it will allow you to distribute your brain across the company (and can then create Evergreen Flows on how to execute decisions).

Before you create Evergreen Flows for every type of decision you make, we need to define the clear distinction between your gifts and your skills. A skill is something that anyone can pick up through training, repetition and practice. A skill can be improved. A gift or talent, however, is not so easily duplicated.

Harvard Business Review outlines[4] the difference as *explicit* and *tactical* knowledge. Explicit knowledge being something we can easily write down and document (our Evergreen Flows). Tactical is a bit more of a nuisance since we quite can't easily put our finger as to *why* or *how* we do what we do, we just *know* what to do through experience and our own insight. This is why we focused on setting the stage, to create environments in our company where your team can learn from your behaviors and through

---

[4] Hagel III, John & John Seely Brown. "Help Employees Create Knowledge — Not Just Share It." *Harvard Business Review*. 15 Aug. 2017

frequent interactions and repetition, can arrive to develop their own tactical knowledge.

Over time, through your constant repetition and training your current and future company leaders on how to effectively lead, you will find that the quality of their decisions and performance will improve. You'll notice, however, that your team may not always be at the same level of output or performance as you are. I do not suggest you wait until your team is at the same or higher level of performance as you, that will just drag on more time. Rather, I suggest you measure through performance metrics and feedback loops what level of performance is the **minimum level of acceptability**. This is not to lower your standards or quality, ever. We just need to understand what baseline your team must surpass in order for their output and performance to be acceptable to your company and your customers.

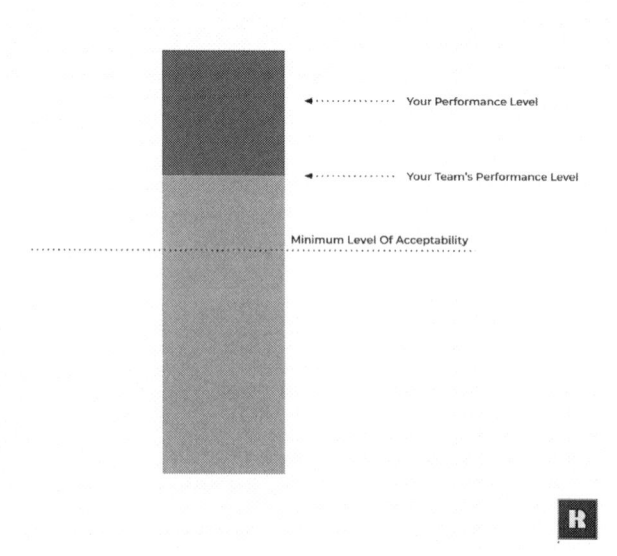

Allowing your team and future leaders to have the freedom and autonomy to lead themselves sooner rather than waiting until they surpass you, gives you the time you need to nurture and foster their needs so they can grow at a more rapid pace. Your time invested in nurturing the future leaders of your company is your investment to your impact and legacy that will live on without you.

Facilitating Movement

As a leader focused on our mission, we have an internal drive, a fire, to move constantly towards our goals. We harness this fire and translate that into our actions in our every day work. As a heroic leader, you must create this fire in your teams so you all move together with the same drive and tenacity. You do this by relentless focus on your company's mission, vision, and values as discussed in Chapter 4 and living out those values in your dealings as a company with your customers, shareholders, partners, and community. As you may have come to the conclusion in this book, it is not simply one thing that will drive you and your company towards higher levels of success. It is the combination of all the things we have covered, simultaneously working together in harmony, and lead with a constant drive and focus by you at the helm of your company.

Your habits of constant team communication, touch points, and feedback loops allow you to iterate quickly when needed and make faster decisions, all the while constantly feeling the pulse of your company's cadence and growth. As you scale, your communications too must scale. That does not mean that the number of communications increase but rather you hone in your communication with key people on your team. Here enters your autonomous task units. Every company is unique and yours is no exception. So within your team hierarchy you have to identify the leaders you have within your company. Your leaders can be for specific departments or initiatives. Depending on your company, you will have a certain number of leaders. Nevertheless, three of those leaders must be the heads of your operations, marketing, and product/service fulfillment departments.

With your company leaders it is important that you have clear and established lines of centralized communication and regular standing meetings. Meetings are worthless unless you do them right. There are countless books on the subject and giving general advice here is not beneficial to anyone, so I will just give you examples of the two types of meetings I hold.

The first are weekly 80/20 meetings to discuss the coming weeks top priorities and initiatives. This can be an all team meeting or a department by department meeting. The meeting agenda follows its title: what are the 80/20 priorities this week, who needs to do what, what resources do you need, and what needs to be facilitated to drive action.

The second type of meeting I hold are power meetings which are quick 15 minute collaborations with specific leaders or departments to keep the momentum going from our 80/20 meeting or address questions that have come up along the way. When meeting with your team, keep in mind that you have to splash in your culture and keep a positive team relationship. That goes without saying.

As the key driver in your company's growth, you must be sure to include a select time block during your week to lead these meetings and ensure you have ample time for your 80/20 key actions. Review Chapter 6 if you need to refine and optimize your day and week to accommodate your team communications.

ACTION MAP

1. *Write out 5 ways you can adapt to become or improve upon being a heroic leader. Detail out when and how you will implement them.*

2. *How do you define the way you do business?*

3. *What behaviors do you want your team to exhibit and learn from you? How will you teach them?*

4. *List out the key feedback loops and data you need to monitor in order to keep the pulse of your company:*

5. *Who will you go-to for a sanity check?*

6. *Who are the current and future leaders in your company and how are you nurturing their growth?*

7. *What are the minimum levels of acceptability in every key area of your company?*

8. *How will you facilitate movement in your company?*

9. *Check your daily time blocks and detail when and where you will hold your 80/20 team meetings and power meetings. You control your calendar. Try to limit others from manipulating your time blocks.*

Chapter 10
Orchestrating Your Growth

In the beginning, with all these moving pieces, it will take time to get the engine rolling. But as you continue to move consistently, steadily, things will start to fall into place. There's a simple mental model I draw out for my clients that shows how taking action over time will lead to results. But how much action is necessary and how long will it take to see progress or reap the rewards? Using the Fibonacci Sequence backwards, we can create a simple mental model to understand the importance of implementing now (action) and maintaining our momentum (consistent action).

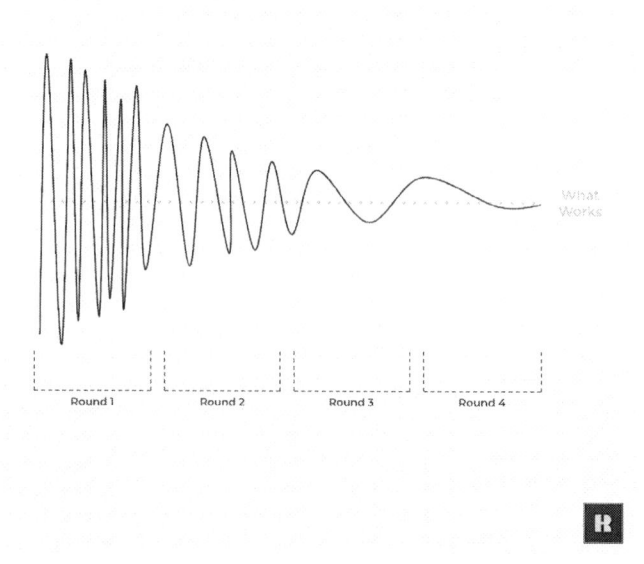

Perhaps the first round of implementation will take you 21 attempts or actions before you start to see any momentum. Then you go back to refine your approach by taking what you learned through your feedback loops and measurements. Round two may then take 13 attempts. Round three, 8. Round four, 5. Until you get to a place where things just work and you're maintaining a cadence that will be the new baseline for your company's future. Remember, we are in it for the long term.

With your team working with greater clarity and in synchrony, with you focusing on your highest leverage activities, the journey to reach your new levels of success will be invigorating. Your journey matters. Your team's experience matters. Your impact matters.

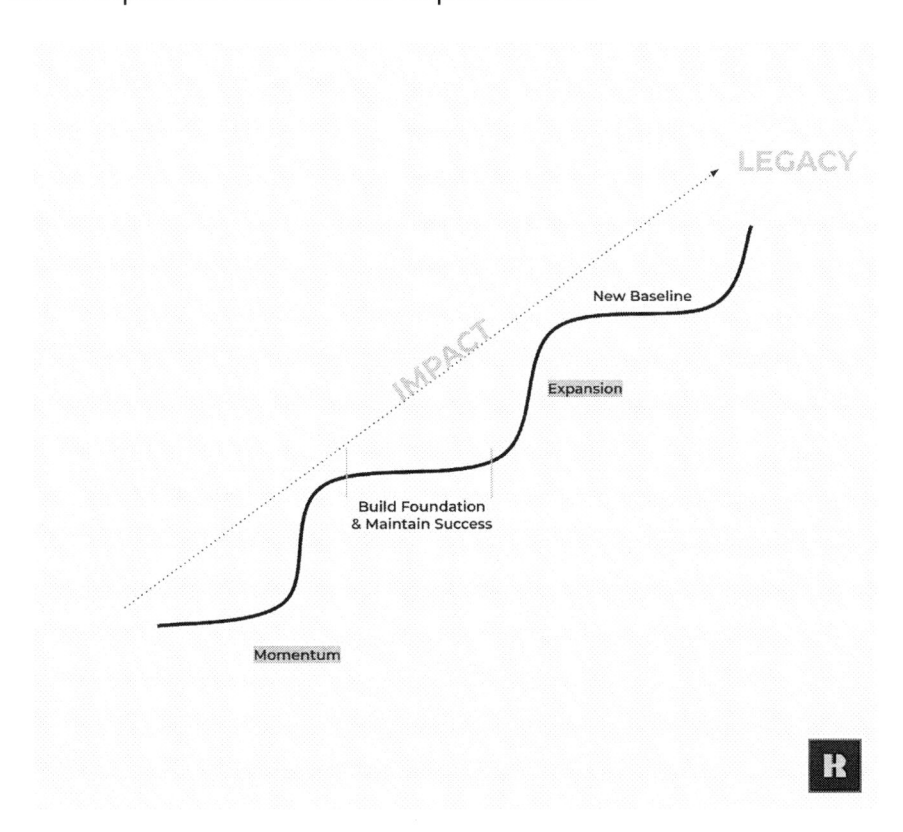

What does impact mean to you?

Your impact began with you, when you said "yes".

Like wildfire, it spread to your family, friends, and steeped into your community.

It allowed you to serve your clients and, now, serve them at a much higher level. Expanding your impact to your team, shareholders, partners, global community...

Productive Profits™ doesn't just mean more profit for your bottom line but profit that changes lives.

Now that you are able to have a clear guide to continue to expand your impact, your work has literally just begun.

Reaching new horizons and continually raising the baselines allows you to expand to levels you may not have thought of when you started. Momentum compounds momentum and opportunity compounds opportunity. With the leverage of being in a position where you are driving the mission forward, you can seek, explore, and do more of what is possible.

Leading you to leave the legacy that you were created for. The legacy for your clients. For your team. Community. Friends. Family.

It is my honor to be a part of your journey.

Do Good Work,
Raul